THE MONSTERS IN OUR CLOSETS

THE MONSTERS IN OUR CLOSETS

Secrets to Healing the Psyche

Virginia Novak, LCSW

BLINKING LIGHT PUBLISHING

TUCSON • ARIZONA

Blinking Light Publishing Company
P.O. Box 27503, Tucson, Arizona 85726-7503

Library of Congress Catalogue Number: 200791096

ISBN-13: 978-0-9799643-0-5

Printed in the United States of America.

This book is dedicated to all those who are
so trapped by their pain that they struggle
to laugh, love, or live.

CONTENTS

———————————— *Chapter One* ————————————

THE ORIGIN OF MONSTERS   3

———————————— *Chapter Two* ————————————

AVOIDANCE AND STORAGE: THE PSYCHE'S CLOSET   21

———————————— *Chapter Three* ————————————

A SNAG WITH STORAGE   29

ACKNOWLEDGEMENTS

Faced with the task of listing everyone who deserves thanks for their help with this project, I am filled with sympathy for all the award winners who must read through their long laundry lists on national television. Unfortunately, there are not many ways to do this, so...

To those without whose help this book would not exist: first and foremost, the wonderful Judith Glixon, who supported me when I needed it most and who saw this book through the early, most difficult, formative stages; and the truly amazing Tanya Jarvik, whose skills as an editor are without peer and who saw this book through the final, most difficult, concluding stages. To all those who helped this little critter along the incredibly difficult path between, especially Pam, Patricia, Jean, Mark, Andy, Tina, and Elizabeth. And to the tremendously talented Jim Pipik, whose artwork graces the cover; the busy and brilliant Lisa Cooper Anderson, who put her entire life on hold to typeset this tome; and my wonderful cover designer Zorbabel Leon. Thank you, one and all, from the bottom of my heart.

I'd also like to thank all those without whose help I would not exist. To all my friends and family: your support has meant the world to me. And a special "thank you" to my parents, who taught me to question authority. You made it possible for me to see beyond the box of conventional theories. To Mary, my guardian angel—it's been a big job over the years, but you've handled it well. To Nancy, my mentor: I can't thank you enough for your guidance, advice, and assistance. And to Drew—your support and encouragement over the past few years have helped me more than I can say.

I also need to thank those who have most influenced my professional thinking. First, to Francine Shapiro, Ph.D., whose bravery and determination as an innovator have made the importance of integration clear to so many. And my clients, who have been my greatest teachers: your openness, courage and strength inspire me daily.

And finally, to the Divine Light, without whose guidance, support and assistance neither I nor this book would exist.

—TGBTG

INTRODUCTION

I n recent years, certain medications have been vigorously promoted as an effective solution for various psychiatric disorders. At the same time, little to no attention has been given to innovations in the treatment of emotional problems caused by life events. For many people, this unfortunate combination of factors has created the mistaken impression that emotional problems are primarily caused by brain chemistry and that life experience has little effect on mental health—*The Monsters in Our Closets: Secrets to Healing the Psyche* is an attempt to rectify this state of affairs. By drawing together breakthrough explanations of how experiences contribute to the development of emotional disorders, this book explores the connection between life events and dysfunctional reactions and looks at ways to prevent and treat those reactions.

While it may seem impossible for one relatively small book to explain the cause, treatment and prevention of so many mental health issues, a few critical concepts tie these various topics together and make them surprisingly understandable. Just as a puzzle becomes easier to assemble when the picture is obvious, these explanations of the psyche's underlying dynamics simplify the puzzle of mental health. Rather than dissecting particular disorders or examining specific theories, therefore, *Monsters* will explore the bigger picture of emotional health—the overall workings of the psyche and the few glitches at the foundation of a wide variety of psychological symptoms and processes.

For some people, these generalizations about the impact of life events might seem presumptuous. After all, controlling one's feelings is often seen as an extension of free will, and the suggestion that emotional problems can, to some degree, be anticipated seems to infringe upon this right to self-determination. As a result, certain readers might be offended by the inference that they are susceptible to the same psychological vulnerabilities as everyone else, or they may take exception to the inclusive terms "we" and "our" in describing negative reactions—as if they were universal.

Given our willingness to accept common human limitations and attributes in other areas, however, it is somewhat strange that readers may be suspicious of generalizations about emotional reactions. After all, no one would argue that telling children that they cannot fly is stifling their individuality. Most of us would think it foolhardy to "wait and see" if a broken leg will heal on its own. Yet these kinds of tactics seem acceptable when it comes to emotional issues. The idea that "you never know how someone will react" to a traumatic or painful situation is rampant in our culture.

However, it will soon become apparent that this point of view is no more accurate in regard to emotional health and psychological makeup than it is to physical health. Once we understand the basic rules governing the psyche's functioning, we will see that emotional problems caused by life events are surprisingly predictable. Just as we have all learned that "flying" off the roof of a garage never succeeds and often results in injury, we will come to realize that emotional and psychological problems follow certain foreseeable and common patterns. This book is about those patterns and about the human psyche—our psyche—as a functionally consistent entity. It is indeed about *us*.

DISCLAIMER

The Monsters in Our Closets offers a theoretical model regarding the nature and treatment of a variety of emotional problems. It is a general guideline regarding the overall workings of the psyche and is not meant to address the specific emotional issues and disorders of the reader. It is sold with the understanding that the publisher and author are not providing counseling services. If professional psychotherapeutic assistance is needed, a competent, trained counselor should be consulted.

DO NOT ATTEMPT ANY EXERCISES WITHOUT READING THE FOLLOWING:

This book focuses on events that overwhelm our ability to cope and contains exercises for those readers who are in counseling. Many exercises involve thinking and writing about disturbing events that have occurred in the past. These tasks can bring up very painful feelings that may be hidden from awareness by a "dissociative" barrier. Completing the exercises in this book is like walking on thin ice that can give way at any time. Readers who are not currently in therapy SHOULD NOT COMPLETE THE EXERCISES. These exercises should only be attempted with the express permission and assistance of a professional counselor.

THE MONSTERS IN
OUR CLOSETS

Chapter One

THE ORIGIN OF MONSTERS

When we remember that we are all mad, the mysteries disappear and life stands explained.

—Mark Twain

When confronted with the term "emotional problems," we probably envision such dramatic examples as explosive rage outbursts, disabling panic attacks, flashbacks of dreadful childhood abuse, or serious drug addictions. These "Godzillas" of the psyche, with their talent for thoroughly demolishing lives, certainly do demand attention. However, many smaller demons lurk in the dark corners of the psyche as well: low self-esteem, temper flare-ups, uncontrolled stress, lack of assertiveness, and dysfunctional relationships to name a few. While these little beasties seem comparatively minor, they still play a significant role in our emotional struggles.

Smaller monsters cling to us and stunt our emotional growth, interfering with our ability to maintain stable relationships, raise healthy children, and succeed professionally. Worst of all, because they are easily disguised by the psyche's subconscious defenses, they often go unrecognized for years, decades—sometimes, even a lifetime. Without explosive symptoms to signal their presence, these tenacious little creatures flourish in dismissive lack of attention and slowly

3

destroy life's joy and triumphs. While behemoths, such as drug addiction and severe mental illness, are indeed devastating, all the psyche's monsters—big and small—have the capacity to do tremendous damage.

Luckily, it is now possible to rectify and even prevent some of this damage. Recently, for example, psychiatric disorders that are generated by chemical imbalances have become much easier to recognize and correct. However, disorders caused by life experiences have proven to be more challenging. Historically, we have had trouble seeing the connection between life events and emotional problems and have not understood the origins, composition and vulnerabilities of monsters produced by life events. As a result, they have been free to strike at will, often taking us by surprise, and we have settled for conquering symptoms and using erratic treatment options. Without a cohesive plan of attack or the ability to root out underlying issues, we have been left shooting in the dark.

But no longer! It is now possible to see the true—and remarkably simple—nature of these beasts. As rudimentary as it may sound, the reason life events cause emotional problems is a basic glitch in the psyche's normal assimilation of experiences. In reality, monsters of all shapes (from rage outbursts to addictions) and sizes (a persistent case of the blues to colossal depression) are often rooted in this ordinary malfunction. Rather than being random, rare occurrences or separate, distinct disorders, these monsters are incredibly common and become surprisingly easy to anticipate, resolve and even prevent once we are familiar with how they function. At last, there is a way to bring our psyche's monsters into the light and break the grip they have had on our lives.

STEPPING STONES AND STUMBLING BLOCKS

As a child, I remember looking at adults and thinking they were weird. They were never happy. Even when they should have been having fun, they didn't seem to really be there. They all appeared mutated somehow, and I remember resolving that I was not going to be like them. But as I got older, I picked up as much baggage as everybody else. I can't concentrate. I have a stack of bad habits and temper problems. I hate it. I've grown up to be exactly like everyone I used to think was weird.

—*Lisa R.**

For centuries, we have known that human beings develop emotional problems for only two basic reasons: nature (the biochemistry and structure of the brain) and nurture (life experiences). The specifics of how nature and, more importantly for our purposes here, nurture affect emotional health is the real question. Usually, this question is discussed in terms of how catastrophic events—serious abuse, devastating loss, major traumas—affect us. It is a knee-jerk reaction to connect horrific experiences with emotional problems. We naturally assume that only true atrocities can have a real ongoing effect on our emotional health. However, smaller events can also be devastating. If we were to honestly delve into the experiences that trouble us most, we would undoubtedly find not just big traumas but also many painful, but relatively common, events. Almost everyone has been scarred by a dreadful breakup, mistreatment by a schoolyard bully, an atmosphere of conflict at home, or other difficult experiences that happen to us all.

One reason we have trouble making a cause/effect connection between these commonplace events and our emotional problems is that experiences do not affect us consistently. In fact, they can have vastly different outcomes depending on our individual emotional make-up and situation. Even very traumatic ordeals like abuse, assault, or rape can become healthy, productive parts of our identity under the right circumstances, while relatively minor incidents can cause enduring damage. This inconsistency in our reactions to events makes it seem impossible to predict how, when and why they will affect us. However, the impact of events is not as random as it seems. A pattern begins

_____

* Unless otherwise noted, the first-person statements throughout this book are either direct quotations—used with permission—or compilations of comments made by several individuals. In all cases, the names and identifying information have been changed.

to emerge when we look at whether or not experiences have gone through *integration*—a critical function of the psyche.

At its core, the process of integration is a way of metabolizing information. Just as the stomach metabolizes food into energy, the psyche processes experiences into productive facts. After we go through an experience, the psyche strips off the residual negative emotions that cling to the memory, learns pertinent lessons, and stores the resulting facts in the appropriate file of our memory bank. The data can then be retrieved later, when the information is needed or when we are trying to expand our understanding of a particular topic. As a result of integration, the experience becomes part of the fabric of our life. Regardless of how painful the event itself may have been, integration turns it into something we can learn from and view as a meaningful piece of our history.

However, sometimes an event overwhelms our psyche's processing abilities. Since this processing failure means that the painful thoughts and feelings are not cleared away, the damaging qualities of the unprocessed incident linger and continue to affect us. Like a limp caused by an untreated broken leg, an unprocessed experience leaves a negative imprint on how we think, feel and act that is very difficult to change. Rather than helping us grow, it interferes with our ability to respond in healthy ways. In other words, even something as terrible as being in a concentration camp becomes a productive part of who we are if it is integrated, but an event that is not integrated, no matter how minor, contributes to our irrational moods and self-destructive behaviors.

Of course, minor events are normally much easier to integrate than those as disturbing as being in a concentration camp, and the fact that integration can wipe out the ongoing sting of disturbing events does not restore the dignity, innocence and resources irretrievably lost due to these experiences. However, the knowledge that it is *integration,* not the qualities of the event itself, that determines the impact an event has on our life gives us the hope that we can limit the damage. The details of how that process works are currently understood only in part and involve complex biochemical processes that are well beyond the scope of this book. However, the outcome of that process is easy to demonstrate if we compare an event that is integrated with one that overwhelms processing.

THE PROCESS OF PROCESSING

Billi is driving her car and runs a stop sign. Naturally, she feels anxious. For a few seconds, she wonders what will happen next, and she berates herself for being stupid and careless. However, when nothing happens, her sense of panic subsides quickly. Since she does not have an accident or get a ticket, she goes on with her day.

Tessa also runs a stop sign, but she is hit by a truck, which crushes her car. Pinned down, she is unable to reach her non-responsive son in the back seat. For 25 minutes, she does not know if he is alive or dead, and in a state of rising panic, she repeatedly curses herself for being careless and stupid.

For both of these women, integration will commence shortly after the incident is over. In Billi's case, her psyche should have no trouble working through the anxiety and other emotions connected with running the stop sign. Though integration will leave the awareness that she needs to be more cautious, it removes the dysfunctional thoughts of being stupid and careless. It labels the experience "past" and files it in her memory bank under "bad driving experiences." When she thinks of the experience later, she is aware on all levels that it occurred in the past. The body sensations, emotions, and images do not stay with her. She remembers how it felt, but the feelings themselves will be only a memory.

For Tessa, however, the integration process will undoubtedly not go so smoothly. Initially, she can expect to experience mood swings, sleep problems, anxiety and general agitation while her psyche struggles with its first attempts at integration—attempts that have a very limited chance at success. Without help, her psyche will surely be unable to digest many of the feelings, thoughts and body sensations, so they will stay as they were at the time of the accident. Even if her son recovers completely, the feelings of being trapped, helpless and panicked are likely to remain with her, though with effort she may be able to push them out of conscious awareness. Also, she will probably continue to think of herself on some level as stupid and careless, and shun reminders of that day by avoiding the intersection where it happened or even by giving up driving altogether.

Notice that in our psyche's eyes, unprocessed experiences never really achieve the status of *past*. Emotions, thoughts and sensory data from these events stay in the present tense and can be unceremoniously dumped into our current situation, sometimes coming back so vividly that it seems as if the event is happening again, and sometimes sneaking into the here-and-now in bits and pieces. In either case, we have to expend considerable energy pushing non-integrated data out of consciousness and must stay vigilant to avoid reminders of those experiences. The resulting exhaustion from keeping events repressed and the confusion between old and current data generate a number of common emotional problems, which we will discuss in detail in the next few chapters.

While the various problems caused by unprocessed events are extremely common, their true origins often go unrecognized. Instead, we usually just label our symptoms. Tessa's feelings of anxiety and of being trapped, for instance, might be diagnosed as an anxiety disorder. She might be told she suffers from low self-esteem, negative self-talk, a driving phobia or panic attacks. Her feelings of helplessness, her relentless self-criticism, and the mental fatigue caused by pushing the memory of the accident out of awareness might be called depression. However, in settling for those labels, we are clearly missing the main point that needs to be addressed. Labeling symptoms by identifying problem moods and behaviors is not nearly as important as pinpointing and addressing their cause.

Sometimes, however, we may feel uncomfortable with looking for the cause of problem emotions and behaviors. We might think we are just finding an excuse. Acknowledging that we have been depressed since breaking up with a lover or that our anger started after working for a particularly abusive boss can feel as if we are copping out, but identifying the underlying source of our reactions is no different than determining if strep bacteria are to "blame" for a sore throat. Looking at the real cause of irrational thoughts, out-of-control emotions, and addictions is not intended to simply justify our problem; rather, it tells us the approach we must take to begin the healing process.

MENTAL INDIGESTION

I know that a lot of bad things happened when I was little, but I don't like to think about them. I don't think about any of that stuff. Now that you mention it, I don't remember much of my childhood at all. It's pretty much blank before 17. And I guess I have problems remembering day-to-day stuff, too. Anything I don't want to think about, like a fight with my mom, I just don't. But it's hard for me to remember other little day-to-day things too, like where I put my keys.

—*Jan F.*

The exact reason we are unable to integrate certain experiences is still a mystery. Perhaps these experiences simply contain too much information for normal integration. The brain may be unable to handle all the incoming data, like a child who cannot chew because he has put too much food in his mouth. Or it may be that our mind shuts down when we are exposed to extreme emotions and/or body sensations. Another possibility is that our busy schedules may simply not allow the necessary room to process experiences containing intense feelings. Although the specifics of integration are not totally understood, it obviously takes time and energy. The hectic pace of our lives may simply keep our psyche too distracted and frazzled to finish this difficult task.

There are also clearly times when our urge to avoid thinking about painful overwhelming memories interferes with integration as well. Since integration requires that we think about experiences, at least on a subconscious level, this avoidance of accessing painful memories is a serious obstacle. Our mind needs time to clear away unwanted feelings and learn necessary lessons. With minor day-to-day experiences, such as a simple case of running a stop sign, this reminiscing usually happens without any conscious awareness or effort. Our psyche can recollect and digest the incident without the possibility of the conscious mind interfering in the process.

A painful, overwhelming event, on the other hand cannot be processed so easily. Because the discomfort catches our attention, we become aware that our subconscious is remembering the experience. Just as a stomachache makes us painfully aware of the usually unconscious digestive process, the disturbing feelings from integrating an overwhelming experience force us to remember it. This is why we tend to ruminate about a disturbing experience, especially right after it happens.

Unlike the pain from indigestion, however, the discomfort of integration can sometimes be stopped by simply blocking the memory. We are all familiar with the advice, "Just don't think about it." The reason this suggestion is so common is that it does indeed stop the pain. Unfortunately, blocking thoughts about an experience also ends the integration process. We need to let ourselves remember a disturbing event, so our psyche can clear away the residual emotions, thoughts and sensory information, which allows us to complete the process of integration. This painful process is the only way to keep negative experiences from having a long-term destructive effect on our lives.

Realistically, however, not every experience can be worked through, even if we take the time our psyche needs for processing. Although letting our mind "chew" on painful events makes integration more likely, our processing abilities will undoubtedly be overwhelmed periodically. Recognizing when this has happened and knowing how to respond is thus the best way to keep events that surpass our psyche's normal integration abilities from having a long-term negative effect. If we want to protect ourselves, we must be able to spot the signs that an experience is not being processed and understand the ways an unprocessed experience affects us.

CRITICAL INCIDENTS

Every time I think I've forgotten Mackie's death, it comes back. I'm tired of reliving it. It was the worst moment of my life, and now I get to see it over and over and over. Sometimes, I think I can forget it. For a while, it goes away, but it always comes back. I don't think I'll ever be at peace again.

—Moesha G.

Clearly, we must be able to spot events that surpass our psyche's natural integration abilities if we hope to address the emotional problems they cause, and fortunately, there are a number of ways to do so. The first option is to look at the qualities of the experience itself. Usually, extremely disturbing events are much more difficult to integrate than those that are mundane. Just as a serious cut is more likely than a scratch to leave a scar, very negative events are more likely to overwhelm processing and thus leave behind negative reactions. This, of course, makes sense on a gut level. We expect very disturbing traumatic experiences, such as violent rape or severe abuse, to be out of the ordinary and life-threatening.

In fact, this is the criterion used by the diagnostic guidebook for mental health professionals. *The Diagnostic and Statistical Manual of Mental Disorders*, 4th Edition (DSM IV), says that we have been through a trauma when we have "experienced, witnessed, or [been] confronted with an event or events that involved actual or threatened death or serious injury, or a threat to the physical integrity of self or others." In other words, the technical definition of a traumatic event is one that endangers oneself or others. According to this definition, only the most negative experiences— war, physical abuse, natural disaster, hostage situations, and so on— qualify.

However, the severity of an experience is not always the best indicator of how it will affect us. As mentioned earlier, we do not respond consistently to experiences, regardless of their qualities. Sometimes, awful experiences can have no negative effect whatsoever. Horrific battles do not emotionally scar every soldier; occasionally, even painful sexual or physical abuse can help someone develop a positive, generous attitude. The same life-threatening event that causes one person to go into a lifelong tailspin can be a "wake-up call" for someone else. In reality, life-threatening, violent situations are not consistently damaging. Our psyche responds to them in very different ways.

Furthermore, many experiences that do not even come close to meeting the official definition of trauma can have an ongoing negative impact on our entire personality. Numerous non-life-threatening experiences wound us deeply. Being rejected by a love interest or having a cold, authoritarian stepparent can create emotional scars that last a lifetime. Therefore, the severity of an event may be a good starting point for determining if it will be overwhelming, but it is certainly not the only consideration. In addition to the event itself, there are a number of other issues that can help us establish whether an event has surpassed

---

IMPORTANT
PLEASE READ THE SAFETY PRECAUTION AT THE BEGINNING OF THE BOOK BEFORE DOING ANY EXERCISES!

EXERCISE 1 - 1

All adults, and most children, have had some overwhelming experiences. They may be as simple as a pet's death or as overtly traumatizing as being held hostage. They may include being picked on by a bully, enduring a divorce, working for a nasty boss, or finding out that a lover is cheating. In a journal, write down several events that seem to have left unresolved emotions. Remember that thinking about an overwhelming experience will often make you feel the way you felt when it happened, so with your counselor, discuss ways to deal with feelings that may come up during this exercise.

our psyche's integration abilities—in other words, whether or not we are capable of processing the event without taking the additional steps outlined in the second half of this book.

SITUATIONAL CHALLENGES

Grad school was hell. There I was, a single mom with three kids, working full time and going to school. I was exhausted all the time. I don't think I realized what a toll it had taken on me until a few years later when some friends were reminiscing about the program. What a shock! I could hardly remember anything: the teachers' names, who was in my classes, even which projects I worked on with my friends. It was all gone. I felt like that whole period of my life had just disappeared into a vacuum.

—*Donna B.*

Sometimes, it is hard to tell when we will be "traumatized" by an experience, but certain circumstances and settings increase the likelihood that this will happen. For example, we are much more likely to have trouble integrating life experiences when we are being bombarded by a great deal of information, or when we are being pulled in a number of different directions, as was the case for Donna. High levels of stress and lack of sleep also dramatically decrease our integration abilities. Notice that these are common aspects of life experiences that are often considered particularly challenging, such as starting college or becoming a parent.

Novel situations are also more difficult to process. Being exposed to a great deal of new information at once seems to demand a great deal from our integration abilities. This is one of the reasons childhood can be so challenging. For a child with limited prior experience and coping mechanisms, even a geographic move, a severe thunderstorm or a scary movie can be tremendously overwhelming. However, childhood is not the only time that new situations are troublesome. Adults in a foreign country, or in any circumstance that is seriously outside their normal frame of reference, can have problems with integration as well. This is

13

why novice soldiers in Viet Nam or Iraq are more easily traumatized than "seasoned" veterans. The combination of intense emotions and the lack of similar experiences greatly increases our risk of being over-whelmed.

While the psyche's integration abilities may be able to compensate for these stressful situations when they are not long-term, external pressures that continue for several years, or are an ongoing part of life, will most likely cause a backlog of unprocessed memories. However, integration is not affected just by external situations. Another signifi-cant factor in whether or not we will be able to process an event is given to us at birth: our mind's individual integration abilities. Just as we each have a distinct digestive metabolism that determines how easily our body metabolizes food, our psyche has a basic predisposition for how well it metabolizes experiences—a factor that affects our integra-tion abilities every day of our life.

EXERCISE 1 - 2

Think about the events in your life. Have you had experiences like Donna's that were overwhelming simply because you were learn-ing a lot of new information, or because you found yourself in a new environment? Were there times when you felt overwhelmed as a child because you did not understand what was happening? If so, add these experiences to your list.

LEVELS OF PROCESSING

I've heard it a million times. "Get over it!" My mother, my teach-ers, even my best friend, have all said it at different times, but it hasn't helped. If I'm not brooding about one thing, I'm obsessing about something else. Simple things get to me, haunt me long after I should have left them behind. And it's not just the big stuff, it's everything: not getting asked to the prom, the fight I had with my husband two years ago, my ex-boyfriend cheating on me twelve years ago. How can I still be dwelling on this crap? I feel like my mind is possessed by little gremlins that make me think about trivial junk all day long.

—*Jamaica D.*

As we have seen, the severity of an experience and the external situation are two important factors determining our ability to integrate experiences. Our individual level of processing is the third. This innate level of processing determines our mind's inherent ability to handle events. Some of us are simply predisposed to process events easily, while others invariably have trouble. Although external factors, such as lack of sleep, can have a remarkable influence on this natural capacity, their impact is usually short-lived. Our basic processing ability, on the other hand, stays with us throughout our life and remains relatively consistent.

No one is exactly sure why there are such dramatic differences in the ability to integrate events. It is possible that difficulty processing is due to taking in more emotional data, which would also explain why problems with integration seem more common among those who are unusually artistic and/or empathetic. Another possibility is simple genetics. Recent studies indicate that some people have a smaller hippocampus—a region of the brain that processes memories—which can cause problems with integration. Early childhood experiences may contribute to differences in processing ability as well. Childhood traumas, especially emotional or physical abandonment by a parent, seem to interfere with our innate ability to cope with overwhelming events later in life. On the other hand, childhood lessons that teach problem-solving techniques, including how to manage emotions, often minimize the impact of later painful experiences.

Whatever the reasons for our basic differences, it is clear that the underlying ability to integrate events ranges from very high to very low. For someone with unusually good processing abilities, even life-threatening, terrifying or heartbreaking experiences have little long-term impact. Just as a high digestive metabolism allows a body to handle junk food easily, a high processing ability helps us effectively work through emotions and thoughts from painful events. Although high processors may still have trouble occasionally, they are able to integrate most experiences.

Given some time to complete processing, they will normally show all the signs that the event has been digested. When they think about it, they will know how they felt at the time without being drawn back into those feelings. They will not obsess about the event or find it affecting their behavior. It will be the *past*.

Levels of Processing

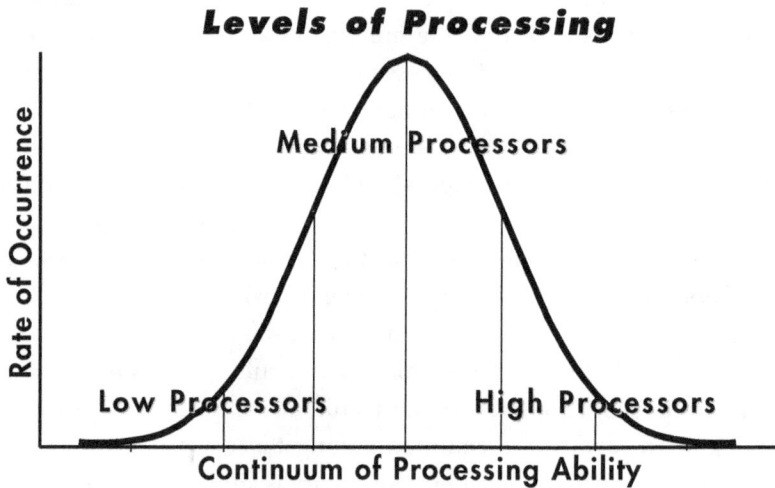

Medium Processors

Low Processors

High Processors

Rate of Occurrence

Continuum of Processing Ability

At the other extreme, someone with very limited integration abilities will often have difficulty processing minor experiences. The most insignificant emotional bump or bruise can leave behind unprocessed painful feelings and thoughts. Since the memories stay fresh, low processors often feel as if they are reliving events over and over. This tendency to become stuck in the past may seem frustratingly irrational to those around low processors, but it is critical to realize that the problem is not due to lack of self-discipline or to being neurotic. They simply have a natural difficulty with processing. Just as those of us with a slow metabolism have to watch our diet and stay active, low processors will need to be diligent about dealing with painful experiences head-on and taking the preventative steps outlined in Chapter Eleven.

As with any continuum, most of us will fall somewhere between the two extremes. In this middle range, we can integrate most, but not all, moderately disturbing experiences. A few "minor" traumas will stay with us, either due to the external factors discussed earlier or simply because

16

the experience hits a weak point in our psyche. As medium processors, we will also usually be unable to integrate most serious traumas. As a result, by the time we reach adulthood, medium processors can count on acquiring a backlog of non-integrated minor and more serious traumatic experiences.

RECOGNIZING OVERWHELMING EVENTS

I know it seems like a little thing to my family and friends. They don't understand why it still bothers me. But it's a big thing to me. I hate the way John treated me. I'm angry, angry, angry, furious! I know that it's been almost 2 years. I know this is ruining my whole life, and I'm not helping myself and nothing's going to change. I know I should be over it. But I'm not. I'm just not!
—Tasha B.

In revisiting the question of which events overwhelm integration and leave behind monsters in our psyche, we now know that serious traumas, like abuse, rape and assault, are highly likely to cause trouble for most of us. In many cases, we also need to consider our brain's natural integration abilities and external situational factors as well. Looking at these three components gives us a rough idea of when we may have trouble with integration and clues us in to when we will need to take additional steps to complete this process. However, rather than trying to anticipate our psyche's reaction to a particular experience, a simpler way to determine when we are being overwhelmed is to look at how we are affected during and immediately after an experience happens. Our feelings, thoughts and behavior at the time tell us a great deal about how our psyche is coping.

In particular, we need to be concerned if we are experiencing thoughts of suicide, a desire to die or feeling as if we are having "a nervous breakdown." These are the clearest indications that our psyche is grossly overwhelmed. (*If you find yourself feeling this way right now, let your counselor or doctor know* immediately.) Thoughts of suicide, a desire to die and a sense of having a nervous breakdown are unmistakable signs that we cannot possibly integrate the immediate situation without help. It also means that these terrible feelings will definitely stay with us on some level even after the immediate situation is over, and that we must be careful during the healing process because the negative feelings can vividly return whenever we confront that event.

While these intense reactions are the clearest sign that integration has been overwhelmed, there are other symptoms that are less dramatic. Some of the most common are problems with sleep and appetite. We will often react with one of the emotional and intellectual extremes, either becoming frantic or shutting down entirely. In other words, we can have obsessive, recurring thoughts about the experience and be emotionally agitated, or we can go the other way and become emotionally and intellectually numb. Notice that the absence of intense feelings and recurring thoughts does not necessarily indicate that the event was not disturbing. In fact, detaching entirely is one of the clearest indications that we have been overwhelmed and that the unprocessed event will continue to affect us in a negative way—even if it does so incognito.

THE POWER IN AWARENESS

> *I feel like I've been living in a dark house, and someone has been going around turning on the lights. It's a weird feeling, suddenly seeing why I've been doing things. Even if I'm never able to change anything, and I hope I will, but even if I can't, it feels so much better knowing that I'm not crazy. There's a reason why I've been acting the way I have, why I've made the choices I have.*
>
> —Katie B.

Many of us have felt, at some time or another, responsible for various irrational reactions caused by non-integrated past experiences. However, the damage caused by our inability to work through life events should never make us feel ashamed. These scars are no more our fault than the physical scars left behind by the cuts and scrapes that happen to us all. This does not mean we are free of responsibility for our emotional health. Just as we can minimize the severity of our physical scars by ensuring that our wounds are properly treated with antiseptic, bandages and stitches, we can also deal with emotional wounds so they heal properly. Knowing our individual level of processing, the external factors affecting integration, and the signs that we are not processing can help us recognize overwhelming experiences when they happen and limit their negative impact.

Furthermore, emotional injuries, unlike the physical variety, can still be effectively treated long after the originating event is over. Even if we were unable to address our emotional wounds promptly, and became scarred as a result, it is still possible to heal those scars years later. Although we were not to blame for how these experiences initially affected us, we are responsible for recovering from those wounds today. In order to do so, however, we must be able to see the scars these events left behind—the changes they caused in our mood and behavior—and know how to undo the damage. Armed with this knowledge, we will be able to conquer our monsters, heal those old wounds and take back control of our lives.

EXERCISE 1 - 3

If you are currently dealing with suicidal thoughts, experiencing a desire to die, or feeling as if you are having a nervous breakdown (i.e., as if your feelings are out of control), contact emergency personnel or your counselor immediately. You must be safe before continuing the exercises in this book. If you have experienced these symptoms during or after an event on your list, be sure that your counselor knows the extent of your symptoms and helps you develop a plan to safely deal with the crises that these memories may generate.

Chapter Two

AVOIDANCE AND STORAGE: THE PSYCHE'S CLOSET

But each day brings its petty dust:
Our soon chok'd souls to fill
And we forget because we must,
And not because we will.

—*Matthew Arnold*

A s we have seen, integration is a critical—if unreliable—function of the psyche. It is the psyche's first priority, regardless of the situation. No matter how awful or overwhelming an experience might be, our psyche initially tries to process as much of the event as possible. This is why the mind often replays a painful event over and over for a while after it happens. Our psyche desperately wants to integrate that experience, but this is not always possible. When our psyche finally stops trying to process an overwhelming experience, we are left with the dysfunctional thoughts, emotions, and memories that could not be worked through.

Over the course of a lifetime, this leftover clutter adds up until we have accumulated an impressive stockpile of unprocessed memories, which the mind locks away using the system that Matthew Arnold

21

described so beautifully above. To accomplish this, the psyche uses the functions of storage (pushing unprocessed memories to the back of our mind) and avoidance (ignoring them). The three complementary functions work together to accomplish the goal of dealing with life experiences. When we are unable to integrate experiences, storage and avoidance give our psyche a way to cope with the unresolved material so it does not affect us more than is absolutely necessary.

STORING EMOTIONAL BAGGAGE

I don't know why they say you can't forget bad experiences. I can. As long as no one asks me about my father and I don't see anything that reminds me of him, it doesn't bother me at all. Sometimes, I can even talk about my mom and brothers and not think about it. I don't like sex, and men give me the creeps, but that thing about not being able to forget isn't true. I did.

—*Jane D.*

Our psyche will continue "chewing" on a painful experience left accessible to our conscious mind for as long as the demands of our life and our tolerance for the discomfort of integration will allow. Eventually, however, it will have to focus on "now," which means finding a way to ignore the old experience. The problem is that an overwhelming experience is by definition one that confounds our processing abilities and leaves our psyche with considerable old data—emotions, thoughts, and information from the senses—which still feel as though they are part of our present reality. In order to move on with our lives, then, our psyche must find a place to put this obsolete clutter so that the old memory is separated from our conscious self.

In order to do this, our psyche creates a storage area to contain the unprocessed information. Like baggage in a closet at the back of the brain, the memories put in storage can be ignored because they no longer interfere with our psyche's day-to-day functioning. After they are placed in this dissociative closet, troublesome memories can stay out of the way indefinitely. Although the memories in our dissociative closet eventually

MEMORY and MEMORY FRAGMENTS

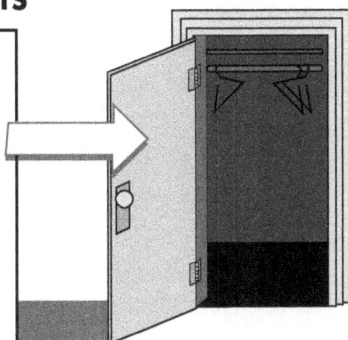

Emotions—guilt, anger, fear, powerlessness, grief, etc.

Thoughts—"I am useless," "I will never be loved," "I am bad," etc.

Sensory data—images, smells, sounds, body sensations, etc.

cause problems if we attempt to overstuff that closet, it is often possible to keep a few memories on hold for decades without a hitch. We can even forget that these emotions, thoughts and sensory data exist unless they are disturbed.

The problem with our dissociative closet is that our psyche is often incredibly conflicted about keeping memories locked away. For reasons we will discuss shortly, memories and memory fragments in storage are surprisingly dangerous, so our psyche tries to connect with and integrate these memories whenever possible while also protecting us from the psychological threat they pose. While we may consciously—and even sometimes subconsciously—want to access the memories and issues that are tucked away in our dissociative closet, our subconscious mind will also use every defense at its disposal to protect us from the danger involved.

EXERCISE 2 - 1

Look at and think about the events listed in your journal. How many bring back childhood feelings that seem strange or are no longer appropriate? Are there overwhelming events you experienced as an adult that make you shudder when you think about them? Put an asterisk next to the experiences that seem most aversive. They will need additional attention.

THE DANGER OF UNPROCESSED EXPERIENCES

Since Mackie was murdered, things just haven't been the same. I have a hard time going outside. Seems like every time I step out of the door, I see someone who looks just like him. And going to that convenience store, where it happened—forget it! I'm still going way out of my way to avoid it. I know it's been almost two years, but I'm not going there. Every time I even think about the place, it all comes flooding back—it's so awful!

—Moesha G.

In order to understand the dangers that stored memories pose, we need to remember that whenever an experience is not completely integrated, unprocessed feelings and memories stay exactly as they were when integration stopped. This can be a difficult concept to grasp. We naturally assume that emotions from past experiences go through transformations. We expect them to change as we change. When we deal with childhood traumas as adults, we anticipate having adult reactions, not those of a young child. However, once a memory stops being processed, it stops changing. The passage of time has no real effect on stored feelings. All the non-integrated emotions and thoughts stay exactly as they were when the event happened.

This means that if we were to access these old memories, we would not only have to deal with the emotions we experienced during the original events, emotions which were frightening enough on their own to be overwhelming, but we would also have to deal with the fact that those emotions make little sense in the context of our current situation. For example, imagine that a young child has the traumatic experience of being lost in the woods for a couple of days and afterwards is unable to process the feelings of being alone, confused, and terrified, all of which coalesced in an overwhelming desire to be found and comforted by his mother. As that child becomes an adult, those childlike feelings are less and less appropriate. When these outdated emotions surface, they make no sense and thus are even more disturbing and threatening than they were originally.

It is easy to see why unprocessed memories are such a threat to our sanity. The combination of dangers that these feelings involve—the original overwhelming emotions plus the sense that what we are feeling is inappropriate for our current situation—is just too much to tolerate. The least distressing option for coping with these memories, therefore, is to keep them in storage. Putting the memories away and developing defenses to keep them buried allows us to carry on with our life. Unfortunately, keeping those memories locked away is not always easy. Storage is not a perfect process, and problems occur for a number of reasons.

Probably, the most common cause of storage failure is the psyche's tendency to make connections between current and past experiences during the process of integration. Seeing patterns in the chaotic flow of our lives enables us to learn critical life lessons. However, grouping experiences in this way means living with the continual threat that a day-to-day experience will "trigger," or make a connection with, a stored memory. Other times, fatigue may cause the storage function to break down. Our psyche can become overburdened from holding on to too many memories, or because life in general is too exhausting and we are simply drained. Oddly enough, a quiet, safe period in our life may also cause events to surface. In this situation, the available resources and our increased energy encourage our psyche to deal with experiences that have been left "on the back burner."

This is where the function of avoidance comes in. Avoidance makes use of addictions—a wide range of which will be discussed in Chapter Five—and various other defenses to protect us from stored memories. Some of the tactics our subconscious uses to protect us from painful

EXERCISE 2 - 2

In order to see how the emotions from overwhelming experiences remain unchanged, think about one of the events on your list. Choose an event that you will feel safe allowing yourself to remember. Remember how you felt at the time. Notice the feelings that you have now. Chances are that you will feel exactly the same as you did originally. The feelings will have changed very little in spite of the time that has passed and how much you as an individual have changed.

memories can be incredibly subtle, even to the point of occurring on a purely subconscious level. Since these avoidance strategies are extremely difficult to recognize, we are often oblivious to their presence—which is a serious problem, because defenses that are beyond our awareness are also beyond our control.

SUBCONSCIOUS AVOIDANCE

> *I picked up the bad habit of not dealing with issues when I was a kid. My usual reaction to problems, such as a fight, was to curl up in my own little world and try to ignore the problem. Well, my strategy of avoidance worked okay through childhood. I could ignore kids that were mean to me and still lead a fairly normal life.*
>
> *But when I got divorced, using avoidance became very costly. So many parts of normal life became unbearably painful. Even being around the friends I had when I was married was too painful. Without even realizing what I was doing, I ended up moving, took on two jobs and never started another family, all because those things brought back painful memories about what I had lost. My world was closing in on me. I spent what little free time I had gambling just so I didn't have to deal with life.*
>
> *—Jim R.*

The human mind is incredibly creative at finding ways to avoid the pain and psychological danger of past overwhelming experiences. Some defenses are nearly invisible to our conscious mind. One such defense occurs when our psyche protects us from thinking about a painful memory by blinding us to our emotional problems. Just as a serious scar will remind us of the accident that caused it, taking a good look at our irrational reactions can remind us of the events that caused them. So to protect us, our subconscious mind does everything in its power to keep us from acknowledging that we have been affected at all. We tell ourselves that we have always had our current personality, and we forget how we felt and acted before the overwhelming event happened.

Another example of our mind's ability to avoid buried memories is our tendency to obsess over relatively minor issues in order to distract ourselves from those that might be more painful. For example, a woman with an abusive father might focus instead on the fact that her mother said something tactless during their last conversation. Even defenses that are relatively straightforward and obvious can at times be difficult to recognize. We may rationalize addictions to work or gambling by telling ourselves that we need the extra money or that we deserve the fun. Our psyche uses these distractions to cover the fact that we are avoiding reminders of painful experiences. It often succeeds in convincing us that, like Jim, we are too "busy" to do anything that might bring up painful memories.

The psyche can seem to act independently in its efforts to keep us "safe" and to avoid the old memories in storage. Because its efforts to protect us are so powerful, we may not be able, on our own, to conquer the drive to avoid dissociated memories. For this reason, the objective opinions of others, especially a counselor, are often necessary to help us see the effects of our history. Discussing our history and reactions openly with a counselor is critical in the battle against the psyche's tenacious use of avoidance. We may also want to explore the possibility of discussing our

EXERCISE 2 - 3

Think about the process you went through when you identified non-integrated events in your life. Did you avoid thinking about certain experiences? Are there others that you still try not to think about? These are probably the non-integrated events that generate the most intense emotions. If you and your counselor intend to deal with these experiences and you have a plan for handling the crisis they may generate, add them to your list. However, be sure that you know what to do if you are in crisis, because even the act of writing these events down can break through your wall of dissociation and bring up very painful feelings.

issues with others who have similar problems, for instance in a therapy group. In certain situations, others' feedback can be very beneficial.

While it is not advisable to dredge up buried memories and deal with them on our own, an awareness of the psyche's mechanisms can be invaluable as we begin the healing process. Understanding how buried memories interact with the psyche to create emotional problems gives us a chance to take an active role in eliminating our self-destructive impulses and out-of-control emotions. Just as knowing whether a runny nose is caused by a bacterial infection, a virus or allergies helps us determine the most effective physical treatment, knowing the source of our problem emotional reactions also helps us find the best and fastest way to recover emotionally.

Chapter Three

A SNAG WITH STORAGE

In the premier episode of Star Trek: Deep Space Nine, *Captain Sisko meets spirit beings who have no bodies and are unfamiliar with the ways of humans. As the beings use the people and situations in Sisko's life to give themselves substance, Sisko tries to explain human concepts, such as linear time and relationships. He becomes frustrated when the image of his wife's traumatic death keeps recurring, and he yells at the spirit beings, "Why do you keep bringing me here?" The beings respond by saying that it is Sisko who is bringing them to that experience. Sisko comes to understand that he has been emotionally stuck in the same spot since her death. Reluctantly, he acknowledges that time is not totally linear after all.*

L ike Captain Sisko, we often find ourselves becoming stuck at points in our lives when we were traumatized or overwhelmed and were forced to use the psyche's functions of storage and avoidance. Though the usual symptoms of being stuck are undoubtedly less blatant than Sisko's, we usually pay a price for using storage and avoidance—not only because the stored memories are psychologically dangerous, but also because the actual *process* of storing and avoiding memories in itself involves risks. Some of the problems happen if the process breaks down, allowing stored memories to leak out; these problems will be discussed in Chapter Four. Here, we will discuss problems that are side effects of merely using storage and avoidance.

EMOTIONAL NUMBING

> *I don't know for sure when I realized how numb I felt. Maybe it was at my wedding. I remember not feeling as happy as I expected. I didn't feel much of anything really. But it wasn't obvious until after I found out I was pregnant with Jack. I just didn't feel like me. I remember thinking that I should have been ecstatic, but I was just there. It all felt unreal. That was when it became noticeable, but it's been going on for years. And it's getting worse and worse all the time. It seems like whenever anything bad happens, I just go blank. And then I never come out of it. I just get more and more dead.*
>
> —*Cecelia D.*

One relatively common side effect of the use of storage is emotional numbing. Numbing is the psyche's way of preventing current emotions from triggering emotions in storage. Although we usually think of emotions as separated from or even in opposition to each other, in reality, our different emotional states are closely tied together. Feelings easily connect with and bring up other feelings. Grief can bring up anger. Fear can become shame. Even positive emotions, like joy and love, can link with painful feelings. For example, a woman having a wonderful time on vacation, sipping a cool drink and looking at the Hawaiian sunset, might think, "Oh, too bad my sister isn't here, she would love this" and suddenly feel overcome by sadness and nostalgia.

However, this is not only true of connections between here-and-now emotions. Feelings about current situations can also connect with, or "trigger," emotions in storage. So fear from a here-and-now situation can drag old shame out of the closet, or current frustrations can trigger buried anger, even when what is happening now has nothing to do with the old memory that generated those buried feelings. For example, the fear of being fired after problems at work can still bring up old fear and shame from a sexual abuse history. Emotions connect not only with similar and dissimilar current feelings but with old feelings, both alike and unlike, as well.

Though the tendency for current feelings to connect with those from the past is usually fairly controlled, there are times when these connections are more extensive and indiscriminate. Usually wholesale triggering is caused by our individual psyche's approach to integration, but occasionally aspects of our daily life—for example, regular exposure to a significant trigger—or the nature of the memories in storage can also make this happen. In these cases, our psyche may choose to defend itself by shutting down *all* feelings. While disconnecting from every emotion clearly has its drawbacks, it is also an incredibly effective way to avoid bringing up pain from past overwhelming events. This method of protecting ourselves from the dangers of triggering works remarkably well.

Like all coping mechanisms, however, numbing comes at a price—a much higher price than we might expect. In addition to simply feeling as though we are going through the motions of life on autopilot—without life's color or joy—numbing also has a number of incredibly serious and destructive consequences. At its most extreme, numbing causes us to reflexively shut down all feelings, both positive and negative. When this happens, the only sensation remaining is a tremendously disturbing sense of emptiness—an emptiness that can be so distressing we may become physically or emotionally self-destructive in order to feel *something*. As difficult as it can be to imagine, those of us dealing with the most severe forms of numbing sometimes prefer the sensation of pain to a total lack of feeling.

Fortunately, this level of numbing is relatively rare, but milder versions of numbing have serious consequences as well, primarily due to their disruptive effect on our intuition. While our "gut instincts" often go unnoticed and unappreciated, they are a critical resource for negotiating life's major decisions, such as those about our career, our relationships or where to live. Consulting our internal compass is critical when facing these momentous decisions, but numbing destroys our ability to rely on this intuition, which in turn can leave us floundering for a life direction, or worse, push us towards a life path that ultimately feels wrong. Numbing and detachment also sabotage our functioning in another way—through blind spots.

EXERCISE 3 - 1

Think about your ability to feel emotions. List a variety of feelings, including joy, affection, anger, grief/sadness, fear, shame/guilt, and the feeling of being powerless or out of control. Next to these feelings, list one or two experiences during which you have had these feelings. The experiences do not need to have been overwhelming. They could be as simple as getting a traffic ticket or as multifaceted as falling in love. Now try to remember how these emotions felt in your body. If you are able to do this exercise without difficulty, numbing is probably not a defense your psyche is using. However, if you have trouble identifying when you had a feeling or how it felt in your body, put an asterisk by this feeling. You and your counselor may want to focus on this issue.

BLIND SPOTS

I still can't believe my mom didn't do anything! It just doesn't seem possible that she didn't know I was being sexually abused. She's a counselor, and I was showing all the signs. I knew all kinds of things about sex. She even walked in on me one time when I was doing sexual things with my dolls. I know she saw, but she just turned around and walked out as if nothing was happening. I begged and begged her not to leave me with him, but she didn't listen. What was wrong with her? Didn't she care about me?

—Jessica W.

Feelings help us to connect with other people. Obviously, if we are detached emotionally, we have difficulty being intimate and loving, but intimacy is not the sole purpose of our ability to emotionally connect with others. These emotional bonds also help us empathize or tune into other people's emotions by being aware of our own. Just as a tuning fork will resonate at the same frequency as another tuning fork in the

32

vicinity, we pick up on another's feelings by sensing them within ourselves. When functioning well, this ability to pick up on other people's "vibes" gives us information about who they are and how they are feeling.

Buried past experiences, however, can seriously interfere with our ability to pick up on this information. Because keeping old memories from surfacing is our psyche's first priority, we will not be able to see emotional reactions or qualities in others that remind us of those buried past experiences. Our psyche blinds us to these emotions and characteristics in those around us due to the threat that they will trigger buried memories. Although this ability to go blind to a potential trigger helps us keep those memories buried, it can also put us in danger. For example, a little girl whose father had episodes of violent anger may have trouble as an adult seeing that a new boyfriend is a very angry man. In cases like this, blind spots make us miss the warning signs that certain people and situations are dangerous, inadvertently putting ourselves and those we love—like our children—in jeopardy.

It may be hard to believe that we could fail to protect our children simply due to a subconscious coping mechanism, but this is a very common problem. Repressed feelings and memories from childhood abuse frequently interfere with a parent's ability to see the indications that his or her child is being abused or warning signs that someone is a potential perpetrator. Even the most loving parent can be surprisingly oblivious to the possibility that a child is being hurt if considering this possibility means confronting buried memories of childhood abuse. For example, a mother who was abused as a child may consciously want to protect her children, and she may devote considerable energy to teaching them about buckling their seatbelts and looking both ways before crossing the street. Ironically, however, she could easily have a subconscious blind spot that prevents her from seeing the very warning signs that she should recognize from her own experience.

Blind spots also have an enormous impact on a child's relationship with the non-abusing parent. A child whose safety is being ignored often feels heartbroken and deserted. Being betrayed by the perpetrator is bad enough, but when the child feels emotionally abandoned by a non-abusing parent as well, the hurt is compounded. Some of us may know how this feels firsthand. If, like Jessica's mother, a parent refused to acknowledge our abuse, we may feel horribly confused, angry and hurt. We may wonder if he or she loved us at all, especially if our parent said that the abuse was exaggerated, imagined, or even that we were to blame.

However, a parent's refusal to acknowledge abuse is often due not to lack of love but to his or her own history. Refusal to acknowledge abuse can be completely beyond that parent's conscious control. Ignoring painful situations is a lifelong habit that leaves a huge backlog of stored feelings and memories. Tuning into a child's abuse would bring up those old devastating feelings. Like tearing down a dam, tapping into backlogged memories would produce a flood of painful emotions. Our parent's psyche will often simply not allow that to happen.

Although emotional abandonment still hurts regardless of the cause, it sometimes helps to know that our parent's behavior may not have been deliberate. At one time or another, we have all felt powerless in the face of our subconscious need to take evasive action. Parents with emotional blind spots are also responding to uncontrollable subconscious defenses. They are using the same coping skills that they used to survive their childhood. While we still have the right to feel angry and hurt, understanding the mind's tendency to develop blind spots can help us separate a non-abusing parent's behavior from the question of whether or not we were loved and to put those evasive actions, and any other destructive symptoms that our parents may have displayed, in perspective.

On the other hand, if we are currently a parent of young children and have a history of childhood abuse, being conscious of our own desire to avoid triggered memories is important. Recognizing this pattern can mean the difference between protecting and endangering our children. When we understand how the mind protects itself, we can be alert to this possibility and work harder to stay tuned in to our children. We do have an option regarding whether or not we stay connected with our children emotionally, and being cautious about our own tendency to have blind spots will help.

RECURRING TRAUMAS

How is it possible to be that stupid? How can I have allowed myself to be raped four times? Once, even twice, I can understand, but four times? And guys treat me like I'm a slab of meat all the time. Do I have "Victim" written on my forehead? I don't get it. My mom says I'm a slut, and I have it coming. Maybe she's right.
—Barb T.

Blind spots and emotional detachment endanger not only our loved ones but us as well. The impulse to keep old data from surfacing eliminates our ability to use emotions to recognize threatening "vibes" from others and to see clues that we are in danger. As a result, like Barb, we may not realize when a situation is seriously hazardous. Blind spots, therefore, are similar to taking the batteries out of an overly sensitive smoke detector. Disconnecting a detector that screams every time the oven is turned on may seem reasonable, but shutting that alarm off puts us at risk of dying in our sleep if there's ever a fire.

While blind spots put us at risk in a general way, a particular risk is that we will repeat past traumas under their influence. Though we normally think of painful times as learning experiences and the worst traumas as our greatest lessons in what to avoid, blind spots can actually reverse this pattern. Because our psyche is most threatened by the feelings connected with our worst traumas, we are more likely to be blinded to feelings and situations that trigger these memories. Like Barb, we may find ourselves mentally disconnecting at the very time that we should be tuned in to every detail going on around us. As a result, we repeat the exact trauma that bothers us the most rather than avoiding it.

This tendency to repeat past traumas is especialy intense in our intimate relationships. Intimate relationships connect us with our deepest feelings and wounds, so romantic partners are, by definition, more likely to trigger past traumas, and as a result, we are more easily blinded to the negative aspects of potential romantic partners that are most likely to call up these past traumas. At the same time, the subconscious urge to resolve those unprocessed emotions may even draw us to someone who will trigger those memories. This is why so many of us find ourselves involved with an exact duplicate of an abusive parent or with the same abusive partner over and over: the name, face, and other external details may change, but the relationship dynamics can stay remarkably constant.

Not everyone who has experiences and emotions in storage, or "on hold," detaches emotionally, but it is always a possibility. Those who have a sizable backlog of overwhelming memories may find it helpful to ask the following questions: Do I tend to minimize the danger in problematic situations? Are those I trust concerned about my choices or my relationships? Do I often repeat destructive patterns from my past? Do I take unnecessary risks? If any of these things happen frequently, it is likely that blind spots are to blame. In those situations, recognizing the presence of these blind spots is essential for our safety and the safety of those we love.

However, learning to recognize our psyche's blind spots will do more than help us avoid future damage; it can also give us information about buried memories that need to be addressed during the healing process. By looking at our psyche's refusal to acknowledge certain issues, we gain insight into the kinds of issues that are in our closet and inaccessible to our conscious mind. For example, if we repeatedly miss seeing that potential partners are angry and dangerous, we can be fairly certain that we experienced a traumatic event involving someone who was angry and dangerous. Or, if we have missed obvious clues that our child was being abused, we need to consider the possibility that we have abuse in our history (notice that this is not necessarily true if the clues were subtle). By looking at the issues that our mind does back flips to avoid, we can identify the areas that may need to be addressed in our recovery.

EXERCISE 3 - 2

Think about the last time that you were in danger. How did your body feel? Write down these sensations in your journal. If you were unable to identify a dangerous time, or if you did not feel anything in your body during that experience, ask yourself whether you are able to feel fear. If your answer is no, your avoidance of fear may be putting you or those you love in danger. Write down this topic in your journal in capital letters and be sure to discuss this issue with your counselor immediately.

PSYCHIC DRAIN

*I first noticed that I was feeling depressed when I was about fif-
teen, but all my friends were depressed too, so it didn't seem like a
big deal. It wasn't until I started college that it was a real problem.
I felt tired all the time, depressed, and cried myself to sleep. The
student health center prescribed antidepressants, and I felt better,
but five years later the crying spells were back. The antidepressants didn't work anymore. The doctors kept changing my meds
and upping the dose, but it didn't help. When my counselor suggested that I deal with seeing my father hit my mother as a child,
I thought she was crazy.*

—Joanne B.

Numbing and blind spots are two of the most dangerous problems
inherent in the use of storage and avoidance. Another common side effect
of simply using these functions of the psyche is that keeping old experiences buried drains off physical and emotional energy. Storage and avoidance rely on the enthusiasm and vitality that would normally be available
for day-to-day life in order to work, leaving us feeling tired and
depressed. Although we may not immediately notice the strain of storing
and avoiding our overwhelming experiences, we will find, just as Joanne
did, that our reliance on these solutions will inevitably take its toll. Years
of keeping experiences in storage will eventually leave us feeling exhausted and lifeless.

Because we can sometimes store memories for decades before we
notice how drained we are feeling, and because there is currently no reliable way to distinguish between psychic drain and depression caused by
biochemical problems, we may find it easy to confuse the two types of
depression. Moreover, there is practically no difference in terms of how
they subjectively feel. Both usually involve symptoms of lethargy, sadness, depressed mood and sleep problems. In fact, some scientists are sug-
gesting that buried experiences actually cause biochemical changes in the
brain that mirror those involved in genetically based depressions.

However, we may be able to ascertain whether our depression is due
to the use of storage and avoidance or to other causes by exploring how

37

much we have packed away in our closet. If we have numerous buried traumatic experiences piled up, chances are that our depression is due, at least in part, to our history. This is important to know, because depression caused primarily by the use of storage requires a different form of treatment than a purely biochemical depression. While long-term medication is needed for biochemical depression, addressing stored memories is the only truly effective way to resolve the problem of psychic drain. Medication serves the same role in treating psychic drain as an anesthetic does for treating a cavity in a tooth. It helps us cope with the pain while we address the underlying problem.

Although addressing the different underlying issues in these two forms of depression is critical, a combination of therapies can at times also be very helpful. In order to resolve psychic drain, we *must* deal with stored memories. In order to treat biochemical depression, medication is necessary. However, whether we are experiencing psychic drain or biochemical depression, combining both forms of treatment, especially at the outset, can be beneficial. Medication eases the pain of recovery and increases our psyche's ability to do its three jobs whether our problem is biochemical or psychic drain. Furthermore, addressing traumatic memories will not completely erase symptoms of biochemical depression, but it can help ease them, decreasing our need for medication.

UNMANAGEABLE STRESS

I'm 42 years old and hate my life. I'm stressed out constantly, can't sleep. I'm tired and anxious all the time. I don't understand what the problem is. It's not like I've lived a terrible life. I had a pretty normal childhood. Sure, there were the typical ups and downs. The biggest trauma in my life was when I was 11 and my best friend died. I didn't really like school much, and I haven't had much luck with relationships, but then who hasn't had their share of bad breaks? I just can't understand why I feel so on edge.

—Debbie B.

In addition to making us feel drained, avoiding and storing unprocessed experiences also, over time, often add to our stress level. Usually, we attribute the feelings of stress that bother us as we get older to the external pressures of being an adult, but is this realistic? Are adult pressures actually that much greater than those of children and teens, who frequently feel they have the weight of the world on their shoulders? Young children have stressors like being picked on by a bully or going home with a bad report card, and teens experience immense social pressures and must make decisions that will affect the rest of their lives. Certainly, from this point of view, their stressors are the equivalent of anything we experience as adults

So if our external pressures have not really increased, why does life often feel so much more overwhelming for adults? The answer to this question is simple: stress builds up over time, because the psyche needs tension to keep past experiences buried. Physical and emotional tension prevents memories of the overwhelming events from falling out of storage. As the number and severity of memories in the closet increase, the amount of energy and tension required to keep them suppressed also increases. Since most of us go through many overwhelming experiences over our lifetime, this tension adds up, escalating our stress level, until relaxing becomes impossible.

For the sake of illustration, let's imagine that we can chart Debbie's stress level, so we can look at the stress she experienced over her lifetime (see graph). On this chart, we would see that like almost everyone, Debbie started life with a very low level of anxiety. After the initial stress of birth, her first few years were uneventful. Normal stressors, such as hunger, fatigue, and minor injuries, caused only small fluctuations in her tension level, and nothing overwhelmed her integration abilities. Since she was able to process these minor stressors, they did not leave behind repressed emotions or memories, and after they were assimilated, her stress level dropped back down to zero.

However, in second grade, she had a teacher who teased and belittled her, causing overwhelming feelings of fear, shame and rejection. Although the external stress of the situation stopped with the end of the school year and she was subsequently able to process some of her feelings, the remainder had to be put in storage. This caused a permanent

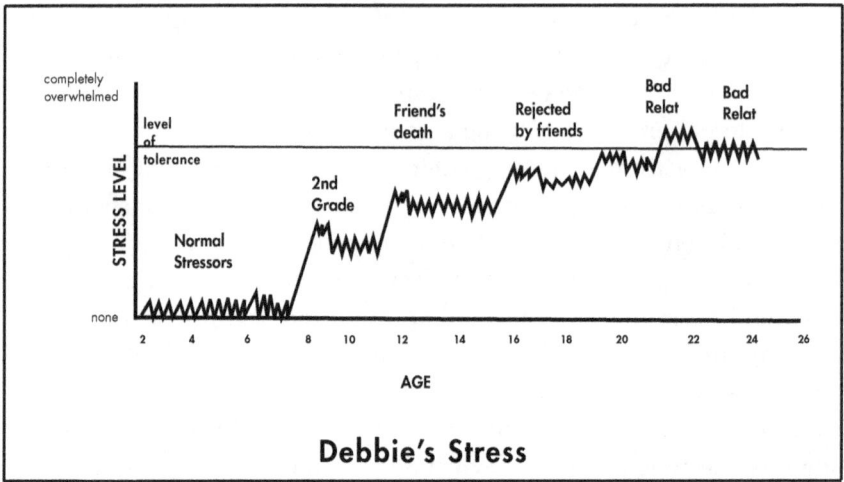

Debbie's Stress

increase in her overall tension level. After second grade, Debbie's minor day-to-day stressors were integrated, but rather than returning to a state of being truly calm, she was forced to adopt the new version of "relaxed." A few years later, when her best friend died, her tension level was elevated even further. After being rejected by her peers as a teen and going through a couple of bad relationships, she was stuck with such an elevated level of stress that she now feels constantly on edge.

Keep in mind that Debbie's discomfort resulted from a life that was fairly typical and mundane. Her family was not overly dysfunctional. She was never beaten, raped, or otherwise severely traumatized—but still, her history of "minor" stored experiences was enough to increase her overall stress level. Since more painful experiences require even greater tension to stay buried, imagine how quickly very traumatic experiences can push our stress level into the stratosphere. Even one or two traumatic experiences can leave us feeling constantly overwhelmed, especially if we have low processing abilities.

CEMENTED STRESS

I was talking with some friends the other day, and I couldn't believe it. Basically, no one was happy. It was such a shock. My

friends and I are making a fortune. We have everything we ever
dreamed of, and we're not happy. I always assumed that once I was
successful, I'd be able to relax and enjoy life. But now I have more
money than I ever imagined, and I can't even slow down and enjoy
it. And it's not just me–it's the same for everyone I know.

Brad T.

Another issue to consider when looking at the effects of stored experiences on our anxiety level is the way this stress compounds other day-to-day stressors. The tension that builds from keeping memories in storage interferes with our ability to cope with normal pressures in the same way that cement interferes with a bucket's ability to hold water. Our mind is set up to accept and process a certain amount of non-overwhelming stress, just as a bucket is designed to contain a specific quantity of water. Life fills our psyche with tension, and integration empties it out, just as a bucket is filled, emptied, and then refilled with water.

Overwhelming experiences are like cement at the bottom of that bucket. Normal attempts to dump out the cement do not work. It stays in the bottom and keeps the bucket from being able to hold as much water as it did before. Similarly, overwhelming events fill our psyche with stress that does not go away. Since this old tension is still present, our ability to cope with normal pressures decreases. Forced to accommodate both the tension necessary to keep past overwhelming events in storage and the

EXERCISE 3 - 3

Think about your level of depression and anxiety, and rate each on a scale from one to ten (one being not a problem at all and ten being completely uncomfortable). If you rated either of these above a five, think back to when these feelings first started bothering you. Were you going through something that might be considered overwhelming? If so, add these experiences to your list of overwhelming events and put asterisks by them. These are some of the events that you might want to consider addressing first.

41

tension of current situations, our bucket overflows more easily, leaving us feeling overwhelmed by even minor stressors.

This buildup of stress from old experiences is one of the most common and troubling effects of simply keeping old events in storage. Along with depression, blind spots and emotional numbing, this type of tension results from the *process* of storing non-integrated experiences. Simply by using the mechanism of storage, we run the risk of developing these problems. Unfortunately, the consequences of storing non-integrated experiences can be even worse. Some of our most destructive emotional responses—the Godzilla reactions that demolish lives—occur when the storage mechanism fails and buried memories are allowed to surface.

Chapter Four

TRIGGERS AND INAPPROPRIATE REACTIONS

At a single strain of music, the scent of a flower, or even one
glimpse of a path of moonlight lying fair upon a summer sea, the
barriers crumble and fall. Through the long corridors, the ghosts
of the past walk unbidden, hindered only by broken promises, dead
hopes and dream-dust.

—Myrtle Reed

Whenever we bury memories, the process of using storage in itself can cause us to become detached, depressed and stressed. This, however, is only part of the story. Although storage is often an excellent way to avoid past experiences, problems develop for various reasons. Storage failures can happen due to fatigue or because our closet is overburdened. Memories are also more likely to surface as we grow older, but most storage failures are caused by the psyche's comparisons between the past and the present. These comparisons happen constantly, without any conscious effort on our part. In a new city, we look for familiar landmarks and recognizable places. Current romances are inevitably measured against those from the past. We bring together related issues, events and feelings so our memories stay orderly and manageable.

This drive to make connections is critical for survival. We would not be able to learn overarching lessons without it, but it can also be incredibly emotionally dangerous. Constant comparisons put us in nonstop danger of having painful buried memories, or fragments of memories, brought out of storage. In other words, the psyche's attempts to consolidate the past and present can "trigger" a vividly detailed memory of a single event or bring pieces of memories—overwhelming feelings, thoughts and sensory data—out of storage one at a time. In either case, these escapees cause some of the most familiar of our destructive reactions. However, before we address triggering, we should briefly visit the incredibly dire consequences of a storage collapse.

FLOODING

> *I learned to "shut down" feelings from my mother. Mom rarely showed any emotion and gave me the cold shoulder if I made the mistake of crying or acting angry. When I was eight, my father died, but I barely shed a tear. Everyone was amazed by how "well" I was taking it. I took this encouragement to heart, and started priding myself on my ability to shut off my feelings by trying to fix whatever crisis or problem arose—right up to the point of my divorce. Suddenly, I found myself unable to recover. Even though I was the one who wanted the divorce, I felt depressed, lethargic and unable to concentrate. It was as if the weight of everything I had put on hold was laid on me all at once.*
>
> *—Ellen B.*

While every version of storage failure causes devastation, most of us would agree that the flood of emotions and memories that is commonly called a nervous breakdown is in a class by itself. Undoubtedly, this is one of the most serious—if relatively infrequent—problems with storage, and usually only occurs when we overstuff our dissociative closet until our ability to keep memories on hold collapses completely. Our exhausted psyche gives up trying to hold everything in, and we are flooded with buried feelings, thoughts and sensory information. Often, we believe that this type of collapse is due to the most recent difficult event alone, just as Ellen did when she pinpointed her divorce. We assume that the entire flood is due to this last experience and fail to see that we have gradually been accumulating a backlog of stored experiences.

This tendency to blame the most recent event can make a nervous breakdown extremely confusing. When it seems that we have "dealt with much worse" in the past, one relatively minor incident does not seem like much of a reason to fall apart. In reality, the backlog of events that caused our collapse was building for a long time. Rather than dealing with those prior traumas, we simply pushed them out of our conscious mind. We packed them away in our dissociative closet. The latest event was just the one that exceeded our closet's storage capacity. In the process of trying to cram in one more painful experience, everything came tumbling out.

In spite of the risks involved in storing painful experiences, however, there is a strong tendency in our culture to equate expressing emotions with weakness, and stuffing them away with strength. While we may admire those who refusal to buckle under in the face of overwhelming pain, we should be careful when confronting tragic situations. Shutting down intense feelings hinders our ability to process them. Unless we face these feelings—either immediately or at a later date—we are not helping ourselves or those we love by being stoic. Although we may believe we are acting heroically by not burdening our family with our tears, stuffing feelings about painful events is simply setting ourselves up to burden our loved ones with even more serious problems in the future.

FRAGMENTS

The car accident didn't seem like a big deal at the time, and I'm okay with most of it, but I really think it affected my ability to love my family. I don't understand why I've been so distant with my husband and kids since it happened. I stopped sleeping with Jim. He rolls over in the middle of the night, and I just hate it when he pins me down with his arm. When the kids want to snuggle, I can't stand it. I feel like everybody's smothering me. They won't

give me my space. Maybe, while I was trapped in the car for all
those hours, I gave up on love or something.

—*Ginnie P.*

While a complete collapse is the most drastic type of storage failure, others are much more common and can be surprisingly destructive as well. For example, the triggering of one intensely vivid memory—a phenomenon known as a flashback—is often extremely painful. Memories that surface as flashbacks rush out of storage, bringing with them all the overwhelming pain connected with those old experiences. Sometimes, this blast of feelings, thoughts and images causes us to feel as if we are actually reliving the distressing event, as if we have gone back in time. At other times, we do not lose touch with what is happening now but feel as if the data from the past has been superimposed on the present. In either case, flashbacks leave us feeling devastated, disoriented and maybe a little crazy, but they are still mercifully infrequent.

Storage failure involving bits and pieces of memories surfacing alone, on the other hand, are astoundingly common. Without a doubt, the majority of problems with storage involve one fragment of buried data—an emotion, a thought or an unexplained body sensation—surfacing alone after being triggered by some aspect from the here-and-now. For example, feelings of fear during an argument with a spouse can bring out overwhelming fear from childhood physical abuse out of storage without any awareness of where that fear originated or even that it is from the past. Or that same current fear can trigger the physical sense of being strangled or the thought "I never do anything right," and in each case, we can have no idea that the triggered data is from the past.

This type of storage failure is particularly destructive because we often confuse the old fragment with a response to the current situation. Flashbacks, while distressing, are obviously from the past, but old emotions, thoughts and sensory experiences that do not include evidence of their origins are nearly indistinguishable from our present-day thoughts and feelings. As a result, we respond as if the old data applies to the current situation, which causes our emotions and thoughts to become exaggerated and irrational. We may even see, hear and feel things that are not based in current reality. These reactions, however, are not as irrational as

46

TRIGGERS AND INAPPROPRIATE REACTIONS

they seem. They make complete sense in their true context: the original overwhelming event.

For example, whenever Ginnie's husband or children tried to be affectionate, the closeness brought up the sense of being pinned down in the car. This sense of being trapped flooded out of storage and adhered itself to the current situation. In spite of her love for her family, their affection triggered that old sensation, which she justified by saying that she felt "smothered" by her family. Clearly, triggered fragments of memories that become attached to a present-day event are tremendously destructive and create a surprisingly diverse assortment of problems, as we will discuss in more detail later in the chapter. There is a way to limit this devastation, however; we can learn to distinguish between past and the present reactions and find ways to deal with triggered data.

TRIGGERS

It's terribly embarrassing to admit that at my age I'm afraid of the dark, but I am. Terrified. And it pretty much runs my life. I want to leave my husband, but if I do, I'll have to sleep alone in our big house all by myself. I can't do it!! Every time I'm alone in the dark, it reminds me of when my mom would play her mind games, trying to scare me, telling me that Freddie comes to get bad little girls. I can't stand the dark. It just terrifies me.

—Elise G.

Every piece of a situation—all the feelings, thoughts and sensory data—can connect with fragments of buried memories. Each of these pieces can be a trigger to bring back emotions, thoughts or sensations from the past. For example, sensory information from the holidays—the sights, sounds and smells—are notorious for bringing up buried feelings and memories from past holidays. Sensory triggers are also particularly problematic for sexual abuse survivors. Buried memories of sexual abuse are commonly triggered by physical sensations, especially during sex.

Thoughts and emotions can also trigger stored pieces of memories. Sometimes, these pieces will bring up more of the same—emotions triggering buried emotions and current thoughts connecting with old thoughts—but they can also unearth other aspects of an experience. For example, thinking "I made a mistake" can connect with feelings of fear or shame from buried overwhelming experiences, or even call up the sensation of being hit. Feelings can also bring up buried fragments. For instance, worry over day-to-day issues, such as feeling a little bit tense about an upcoming test, is capable of connecting with body sensations or thoughts from buried traumas.

However, not all triggers are simple one-shot affairs like those above. One particularly complex trigger is the intimate relationship. Close romantic relationships involve a number of powerful potential triggers. First of all, the deep emotions involved in these relationships are highly likely to generate our most destructive and extreme reactions, and clearly, angry and violent intimate partners can be expected to remind us of prior traumas. However, we may be surprised to find out that relationships with safe, calm mates are also likely to unearth things from our past. Ironically, even the sense of being loved, safe and relaxed that comes from the healthiest relationships can bring old material out of storage, because our psyche attempts to access and process buried feelings when it feels safe and protected.

This tendency of loving, supportive relationships to trigger buried feelings is, not surprisingly, extremely destructive and confusing to both us and those we love if we do not understand the reason for our reactions. In situations where we become angry and paranoid with a loving partner, it is tremendously tempting to find excuses and rationalizations for our feelings. Even when we are tempted to admit that we do not understand why we are being irrational, we may be afraid of seeming crazy. So we might prefer to blame our partner and find some here-and-now reason, however minor, for our reaction—which simply feeds the conflict in the relationship and increases the chance that our feelings will be further triggered.

Fortunately, when we know what is happening and can respond appropriately, the triggering process may actually be helpful to our recovery. As long as we avoid the trap of blaming our reactions on the current situation, triggers can give us information about our history and about how to control our reactions more effectively. For example, if we repeatedly assume that short men are going to be arrogant and dismissive and we had an ex-husband who was short, we can explore the possibility that we found our ex's arrogance and dismissiveness deeply upsetting. This insight into which of our past experiences is being triggered then gives us a chance to use the methods discussed in the second half of this book to control our reactions more effectively and possibly overcome our irrational beliefs about short men.

SUSPENDED CONCENTRATION

> *I was so frustrated. I had been doing great. I knew that I couldn't remember a lot of my past, but I had worked through everything I could remember. I was ready to go back to school, to do better, get on with my life. Then I started feeling dizzy and spacing out. The doctor thought I had ADD, but the meds didn't really help. It didn't seem possible that it was because the stuff I'd forgotten was coming up, but after I worked with my therapist to get to it, I stopped getting dizzy. It was weird.*
>
> *—Genie E.*

The fact that anything—any piece of any situation—is capable of bringing a memory out of storage certainly clarifies why triggering happens so often. In spite of its frequency, however, triggering is still an extremely psychologically disorienting process, because it involves two conflicting drives. On the one hand, our mind wants to consolidate new information with the old material in storage, but on the other hand, our mind does not want to trigger buried memories. These diametrically opposing goals leave the psyche with a dilemma: should our psyche deal with or ignore the connections between past and current information?

As our *subconscious* mind struggles with the dilemma of how to consolidate our memories without bringing up stored experiences, our conscious mind is left on hold. This state of limbo, which feels as though we are simply spacing out, is the first repercussion of memories being triggered. Though it does not happen for everyone, exposure to triggers of very painful memories that our mind desperately wants to keep buried, as was the case for Genie, will cause our ability to concentrate to plummet. We can suddenly feel barely able to function. Fortunately, if this trouble concentrating is a new problem, it will pass after we have dealt with the offending memory.

On the other hand, long-term, serious problems with concentration, or significant gaps in day-to-day memory, such as finding ourselves at work and not remembering how we got there, require special attention. If this happens regularly, we need to inform our therapist immediately so we can receive help in identifying the underlying problem. For most of us, however, triggered bits and pieces of memories are not threatening enough to cause serious problems with concentration. In fact, these fragments often slip from storage totally unnoticed and blend seamlessly with our daily experience—a process that can cause considerable havoc in itself.

SAFETY CHECK

A significant drop in your ability to concentrate is an important warning signal. It is the emotional equivalent of having a high fever. Also, ongoing problems with memory, such as not knowing how you arrived somewhere or having a variety of people tell you that you have done or said things you do not remember, indicate serious underlying problems. If you are experiencing any of these symptoms, tell your counselor immediately.

DISPROPORTIONATE REACTIONS

Socks. I was arrested over not being able to find a pair of socks. I know it sounds ridiculous, but I totally lost it. The neighbors called the police—disturbing the peace—six months' probation and counseling. Boy, was that embarrassing! Though I guess if it wasn't the socks, it was going to be something else. My neighbors were getting sick and tired of my fits. I had them all the time, over the stupidest things. I bet they wondered what the heck was going on at my place—probably thought I was killing someone. I guess I'd rather they think I was beating my wife than know that I was wrecking my house over socks.

—John W.

Any piece of an experience can trigger buried memories, and it is equally true that every piece of a buried memory can be triggered as well. No aspect of a repressed memory is immune to being dragged into consciousness and dumped right into our current experience. Far too frequently, bits and pieces of the past—old thoughts, feelings and sensory information—tumble out of storage and are superimposed on what is happening now. For instance, a childhood sense of abandonment could be triggered by the smell of crayons, or thoughts of being stupid might surface when we see a woman who looks like an abusive kindergarten teacher. These thoughts and feelings are then disguised as part of our current reality.

Notice that the triggering present event does not have to bear any resemblance to the overwhelming event that left the material in storage. Although a similar experience is more likely to bring up old feelings and thoughts, this can also happen when the current and past situations have nothing to do with each other. For example, a current domestic violence situation will very likely bring up thoughts left behind by past experiences of domestic violence, but those old thoughts can also be triggered by anxiety about starting a new job or failing a final exam. In other words, any material from any current situation can trigger old material and cause us to react inappropriately.

Although any aspect of an old event can be triggered and then superimposed onto the current situation, old emotions are probably the most common and the most problematic, especially when they have been triggered by current feelings. Remember that the emotions being brought up were overwhelming in the first place. When these intense feelings are added to the current situation, they escalate our emotional reaction to the point where we may lose control. In John's situation, for example, he probably had a small amount of legitimate anger over not being able to find his socks, but that anger triggered buried rage from past events.

If we could quantify John's anger over old and current events it might look like this:

Stored anger over past overwhelming events:

Current anger over socks:

Current anger over socks triggers buried anger:

Together, they equal a rage outburst totally out of proportion to the current situation:

This kind of extreme reaction would be difficult enough to manage if we recognized that it did not fit the here and now, but the vast majority of the time, we are totally unaware that most of our intense feelings come from the past. This is because the indications of outdated emotions are very subtle. We need to look for these minor nuances consciously in order to recognize them, so we usually miss them altogether. Although a small voice of reason may tell us that we are overreacting, it is entirely too easy to ignore this voice and blame all our feelings on present circumstances. Like John, we find here-and-now excuses for our emotional upheaval.

Excessive emotional responses create some of our most common and disabling symptoms. When buried fear escapes, for example, we experience panic attacks or feel chronically tense. Triggered guilt can cause problems with assertiveness, making us terribly insecure. Repressed feelings of abandonment can prevent us from ending destructive relationships or cause us to avoid relationships entirely. The list of how exaggerated emotional reactions negatively affect us is endless, and the problems with triggered emotions do not stop there. Triggered emotions become even more disabling when they are compounded and deepened to the point that *all* of our feelings fall into the same inappropriate emotional rut.

EXERCISE 4 - 1

We all suffer the effects of triggered emotions in one form or another. Take a moment to think about and make a list of the out-of-proportion feelings that repeatedly create problems in your life. Maybe you are excessively insecure in romantic relationships, at work, or in social situations. Perhaps you struggle with fear of being out of control or vulnerable. Anxiety from past overwhelming experiences may be contributing to your stress level or causing panic attacks. Look for reactions, like John's, that seem excessive, or feelings that you consider so unpleasant that you compulsively avoid them.

RUTS

I feel suicidal all the time. If my kids yell at me, I think about death. If I flunk a test, I just want to die! At first, I thought it had been happening all my life, but in therapy, I realized that it started after I was raped. I know I wanted to die during the rape. And afterwards, I was so ashamed, and angry, and confused, I tried to kill myself. Then, I started feeling that way over little things. At first it wasn't too bad, but after Dave started hitting me, it got REALLY serious. Every time he hit me, I'd dwell on how much I wanted to be dead. After I left him, I thought I'd feel better, but I still felt that way ALL the time. One time I considered killing myself because the mail didn't come—it was ridiculous.

—Sarah J.

In addition to affecting the intensity of our reactions to current situations, old emotions from past overwhelming events increase the likelihood that we will respond with those same feelings in the future. In other

THE MONSTERS IN OUR CLOSETS

words, triggered old feelings affect not just the quantity, but also the quality, of our current feelings. Just as water flowing through a field gravitates to a low point in the landscape and then deepens that area, increasing the likelihood that water will flow along that path again, triggered overwhelming emotions draw us again and again into certain reactions, deepening our emotional ruts until they are almost impossible to avoid.

No matter what the current situation might be, there are many possible ways we might respond emotionally. Often, however, we do not see these various options, because the presence of triggered old emotions makes it seem as if there is only one logical emotional reaction. For example, Sarah might have been angry or just worried about flunking her test, but triggered feelings instigated the feeling of wanting to die. While the tendency to impose old feelings on a current situation is always a nuisance, it becomes a much more serious problem if the current situation is also overwhelming, as the domestic violence was for Sarah. When we repeatedly react to overwhelming events with the same feelings, we store more and more of that particular emotional state and increase the likelihood that it will be triggered in the future. This cycle keeps escalating until we end up having the same emotional reaction to almost every situation.

NUANCES

Before my parents divorced, I was "Daddy's girl." But after the divorce, Dad disappeared. I never saw him again. I was devastated. I felt so hurt and rejected. When I was 8, Mom remarried, but Bob was cold and couldn't care less about being a father. Again, I was crushed. I felt the same hurt and rejection as when Dad left. After a while I noticed that all my relationships with men seemed to fall into this same pattern: I would start out wanting to feel important and end up feeling hurt and rejected. I didn't realize how intense these feelings had become until I was at a restaurant with my boyfriend and he took a long time going to the bathroom. I felt like a little child: alone and unloved. I had visions of my boyfriend sneaking out of the bathroom, getting in the car and driving off without me. I was hurt and felt rejected even though my boyfriend had done nothing wrong.

—Joan Z.

Joan's early experiences with her father created an emotional rut, and her future relationships with men deepened that rut. Her feelings of hurt and rejection when her father disappeared created a weak spot, which affected her future emotional responses. For example, some children with a rejecting stepfather might feel apathetic, and others would feel challenged; for Joan, the past sense of abandonment was triggered, eliminating all other options. Because the incident with her stepfather was overwhelming as well, not only did she re-experience the old feelings, but the intensity of the feeling of being abandoned increased as well. After a few more bad relationships, Joan's feelings of abandonment became so entrenched that they were totally out of proportion to her current situation.

Notice too that the feelings of rejection Joan experienced when her boyfriend left for a few moments retained all their original childlike qualities. She had the same feelings as when her father left, years earlier. Sitting in that restaurant, she felt as though she were a child again and had lost the person she loved most in the world. Because a triggered emotion brings with it all the nuances of the original overwhelming experience, an emotional rut also preserves all these qualities. When a rut is reinforced, all the nuances affix themselves to the new event, regardless of how poorly they fit. Even though the outside situation changes, the emotional reaction does not.

Over time, these reactions become more and more outdated, intense and bizarre, especially when the original event occurred during childhood. Emotional ruts from buried childhood experiences can leave us feeling and acting like little children, causing tremendous damage to our self-concept, careers, and closest relationships. When childhood feelings that have been escalated by a lifetime of overwhelming experiences are dumped into the current situation, they create some of our most irrational and destructive responses. On a more positive note, emotional nuances, like blind spots, give us important information for our recovery. Because they hold information about original overwhelming experience, they can help us identify the underlying stored event that is being triggered.

IRRATIONAL ASSESSMENTS

The night my mom found out my dad was raping me, she acted like a nurse with a patient she didn't like. After she cleaned up the blood, she parked me on the sofa. I sat there trying to figure out what I had done wrong and how I could change it, and I knew there was no way I could fix it. I had screwed up, and I'd never be happy again. The next morning, my mom wouldn't even look at me—barely acknowledged my existence—which just reinforced what I thought the night before.

I went through life convinced I was a screw-up, and my belief in being a failure became a self-fulfilling prophecy. I never completed anything. I dropped out of high school, quit choir, got myself kicked out of dance. I went to six different colleges in five years and still couldn't even earn a two-year degree. Anytime I'd come close to being successful, I'd screw it up.

—Bobbi J.

Although we like to think that our beliefs about ourselves, our relationships, or the world in general are rational and objective, in reality, they are easily corrupted by triggered fragments from past experiences. Old thoughts that are triggered when we make an assessment about a situation are imprinted on and contaminate our current beliefs and attitudes, just like old emotions. In other words, these fragments poison our subconscious thoughts and perceptions about our current situation. The contaminated perceptions then change the way we feel about and react to the present situation.

For example, children normally perceive problems as being their fault. By treating her coldly, Bobbi's mother amplified this interpretation—the belief that she, Bobbi, had screwed things up—which became imbedded in her subconscious. Notice that the timing of this interpretation is critical: a perception becomes most indelible if it occurs close to an overwhelming experience. Like buried emotions, which do not change once integration has stopped, our interpretations are difficult to alter once the event is placed in storage. In Bobbi's case, her mother's behavior on that traumatic night had an infinitely greater impact on how Bobbi perceived the situation than anything that happened months or years later.

Because what we think so powerfully influences how we feel and react, a triggered thought does not just sit idly in our mind. It affects our mood, and the way we interact with those around us, either directly or indirectly. Bobbi did more than just perceive herself as a screw-up. She took direct steps to make this perception a reality. Our perceptions can also take a less direct route. For example, the thought, "People hate me," imbedded during a painful childhood experience, can cause more than just the perception of being unlovable. It also leaves us feeling lonely and angry, which may cause us to become aggressive or to isolate ourselves.

Since triggered old thoughts affect our behavior, they, like triggered emotions, can also reinforce themselves with future events in a vicious cycle that escalates quickly. Unlike triggered emotions, however, triggered thoughts are compounded not by how we feel, but by how we react to, and subsequently interpret, future events. For example, Bobbi's perception of herself as a loser made her give up on challenges too easily, which then reinforced the belief that she was a loser. When our irrational beliefs have painful, overwhelming consequences—like Bobbi's inability to graduate from college—the beliefs that caused those negative consequences are reinforced and strengthened, and the thought becomes even more common.

In time, thoughts that snowball due to further overwhelming experiences can come to dominate our life, especially if we believe that these thoughts are an accurate reflection of reality. As with triggered emotions or full-blown flashbacks, confusing triggered thoughts with a reasonable response to the current situation often makes us respond in ways that are counterproductive or even bizarre. To make matters even more complicated, simply recognizing that a thought is irrational does not necessarily keep it from affecting us. In spite of our awareness, we may still respond reflexively, in the same way that a Vietnam veteran still feels afraid and agitated even though he may know that a flashback of battle is not real. Nonetheless, recognizing the real cause of our self-defeating thoughts is an important first step in overcoming their influence on our behavior.

EXERCISE 4 - 2

Think about the disturbing or irrational thoughts that you common-ly have. Are there any particular thoughts that come up on a con-sistent basis and color your perceptions of yourself (such as, "Nobody likes me," "I'm stupid," or "I always screw up"), other people ("People are mean," "They won't like me if I'm angry"), or the world ("I'll never be safe," "Life is totally random, I have no control")? Do you have stray thoughts that come up under stress (for example, "I want to die," "I can't stand it," etc.)? Make a list of these troubling thoughts in your journal.

SENSORY DATA

> My mom was very critical when I was little and would always tell me that I couldn't do anything right. When I was pregnant, my lack of self-confidence got worse. Leaving the hospital with Donnie, I was terrified. And then Donnie wouldn't stop crying. I tried everything. He screamed and wailed mercilessly. After a while, I learned how to soothe him and he became easier to handle. But I still heard him crying at the strangest times. I would check on him, and he'd be sound asleep. I knew it had to be my imagina-tion, but it seemed so real. Sometimes, I thought I was going insane.
>
> —Dena B.

Although our senses are normally not considered important on a psychological level, overwhelming sights, sounds, smells, tastes, and body sensations are stored, triggered and confused with current feedback in the same way as thoughts and emotions are. Furthermore, although we rarely mistake old images for current reality, confusing other pieces of old sensory data with what is happening now is relatively common. Unfortunately, this kind of sensory confusion can be extremely dangerous. Of particular concern are triggered body

58

sensations, because they can convince us that our health, or even life, is in jeopardy.

Although they may sound like a rarity, residual body sensations—or body memories—are actually relatively common, because distressing body sensations are particularly difficult for the mind to process. Painful accidents, especially those involving life-threatening injuries or burns, often leave behind phantom pain, and incidents involving near suffocation frequently leave behind sensations of being unable to breathe. In fact, any physical feeling intense enough to overwhelm our integration abilities can leave behind sensations that are easily confused with symptoms of serious physical problems.

When doctors are unable to find the cause of these phantom sensations, trying to find treatment is often difficult to the point of being devastating. Since these old body feelings often also bring up painful emotions, searching in vain for help can leave us feeling desperate and alone, completely disheartened by our doctors' inability to eliminate our symptoms. However, doctors are not to blame for being unable to cure physical sensations that are due to the past. Of course, not all unexplainable body sensations are "in our heads," but if we cannot find relief from mysterious pain or strange sensations, we should ask ourselves if these symptoms mimic sensations that occurred during painful past experiences.

Other sensory information, such as smells, sounds and tastes, may not feel quite as urgent, but they can still be problematic. We may wonder, for example, if we are hallucinating. Like Dena, we are used to the idea that hearing, smelling, tasting or physically feeling things that are not there means that we are crazy. While we need to take these symptoms seriously and talk about them with our doctor and therapist, reliving old overwhelming sensory experiences does not mean we are going insane. Re-experiencing smells, sounds and tastes from extremely disturbing past events is no more indicative of insanity than reliving old emotions and thoughts.

In spite of how bizarre they may seem, in the end, triggered sensory experiences are just another example of how buried fragments contribute to our irrational reactions. Even these strange symptoms make sense when seen in the light of our inability to keep stored bits of memories on hold forever. Excessive emotions, irrational thoughts, and unexplainable sensory experiences are simply due to the normal limits of our storage capabilities. However, the limited storage space in our dissociative closets is not the only reason behind our irrational reactions. Problems with the mechanism of avoidance explain another seemingly illogical behavior pattern: addiction.

Chapter Five

LOCKING THE DOOR WITH ADDICTION

I exercise strong self-control. I never drink anything stronger than gin before breakfast.

—W. C. Fields

A t one time, the word "addiction" was used only to describe dependencies on substances, like alcohol and other drugs. Lately, however, we have realized that there is much more to the process of addictions than just physical dependence. We now see that it is possible to become hooked on a wide range of activities and behaviors. In this broader perspective, addiction clearly touches a huge number of people. In fact, it is safe to say that we are all affected by addiction on some level. Whether we experience the effects of dependency directly or indirectly, through family members, friends, or partners, every one of us deals with its destructive consequences. Yet in spite of its pervasiveness, addiction remains something of a mystery.

We even struggle with the very definition of addiction. Dependence on alcohol and other drugs is relatively easy to define, but other than these substance issues, it can be difficult to determine what exactly is addicting. Some non-substance addictions like shopping and gambling are widely recognized, but other behaviors that look a great deal like addiction could just as legitimately be considered obsessions, such as playing video games, watching sports, or scouring the Internet for chat rooms. These behaviors can indeed be incredibly destructive to one's finances, peace of mind, free time and relationships, as many sports and Internet widows will testify. Although it might seem like over-generalizing to place an obsession with Internet chat rooms in the same category as heroin addiction, looking at the entire range of addictive substances and behaviors is surprisingly informative.

In particular, the spectrum of addictions, taken as a whole, sheds light on the baffling riddle of their purpose. Clearly, our current view of addictions has shot down the outdated notion that they are simply meant to eliminate physical cravings for substances. This improvement in our understanding, however, has left us with the puzzle of why reasonable people would give up money, jobs, and relationships, even risk their lives for the sake of shopping, gambling, or having sex with strangers. It is a mystifying question, but a critical one, because it draws our attention to the crucial role that every addiction—big or small, physical or behavioral—plays within the psyche.

We are accustomed to viewing addictions as separate entities. We think of alcoholism as different from gambling, and sex addiction as distinct from codependence. In reality, all addictions fulfill a strikingly similar purpose—a purpose that is less evident in substance addictions but is present all the same. This purpose is the reason our psyche clings to them so tenaciously. Addictions are, in reality, one of the psyche's most reliable defenses, and as we have seen, disabling a defense is easiest when we first understand and dismantle the reason for its existence. Seeing the bigger picture of how addictions work and how various dependencies are connected will make it possible to conquer them in all their incarnations—far more effectively than chasing each down as if it were a separate entity.

PHYSICAL ADDICTION

Rob and I were typical boys. We'd get in a lot of trouble, playing in the gullies, breaking into deserted buildings. It was great, and it kept us away from home, which was important because his dad was a heavy-duty "drink till you're pissed, beat your wife, then drink till you drop" drunk. When we were about 12, we found an old warehouse that was stacked to the gills with cases of wine. So we did what you would expect: we got drunk. This was fun, but the next day, I was ready to do something else. Not Rob. All he wanted to do from that day on was drink. It was weird. In the course of one day, I lost my best friend to alcohol. The last I heard from him, he was 21 and killing off a fifth of vodka before break-fast.

—Jim N.

Of all the different types of addiction, most of us probably find physical addiction to substances the most understandable. Even if we have never experienced withdrawal firsthand, the idea that we can become hooked on certain chemicals is not difficult to grasp. However, physical addictions are not due solely to the chemical properties of the substance itself. For some of us, our physical makeup and genetic predispositions also contribute to the process of dependency. In other words, genetic vulnerability can increase our chance of becoming physically addicted, just as genetic vulnerability heightens the likelihood that we will become diabetic.

Specifically, genetic precursors have been linked to not just one, but two types of alcoholism. "Type A" alcoholism is passed on only from father to son through a very strong genetic predisposition, as was probably the case for Rob. "Type B" involves a less powerful, but still influential, predisposition that can be passed from either parent to both sons and daughters. More surprisingly, physiological issues can also contribute to some addictions that on the surface appear purely behavioral. Gambling and sex, for example, generate specific chemicals in the brain that can be extremely habit-forming. For some people, the rush from these activities is as stimulating as the most addicting substance.

While we cannot make direct changes to our predispositions, knowing the physical side of dependence is an important asset during recovery. When we are aware of the effects of particular substances, our genetic vulnerability, and the interaction of brain chemistry and certain behaviors, we can acknowledge and respond appropriately to these challenges, and we can overcome the tendency to focus on willpower. Rather than feeling weak for having urges to relapse, we can see our recovery in the same terms as recovery from any other chronic illness. Just as we would not beat ourselves up for having diabetes, but would instead focus on the importance of healthy living, acknowledging the physical side to addiction helps us concentrate on healing rather than criticizing ourselves for this vulnerability.

Although physiological issues are an important part of the story of addiction, the process of dependence is obviously more complex than mere physical responses. There are several common patterns seen in addictions which cannot be explained by simple biochemistry. For example, in spite of a strong genetic predisposition and a family history of substance abuse, many people manage to dodge the bullet. Furthermore, it is common for people to "switch" addictions, replacing sex with spending, or alcohol with exercise. If biochemistry were solely to blame, this would not happen. There is another important contributor to the phenomenon of addiction. As with emotional issues, the psyche's response to painful life experiences plays a critical role in the entire spectrum of addictions.

In the past, addictions were credited with functioning only as an anesthetic to the distress caused by events, numbing the immediate pain of difficult times. For example, drinking might be seen as a way to

EXERCISE 5 - 1

Think about the role the physical aspects of addiction play in your life. Do people in your family have problems with addictions? Do you use physically addicting substances—including alcohol and cigarettes—on a regular basis, in spite of the legal, medical, financial or interpersonal consequences of this use? Have you tried to quit previously and been unsuccessful? If so, in your journal, list your use of physically addicting substances, along with your emotional reactions when you have tried to quit, and discuss this issue with your counselor.

deaden the grief and anger caused by a recent divorce, or playing slot machines all weekend as a way to cope with the frustration of a dead-end job. The problem, however, is that this view of addictions does not stand up to scrutiny. Alcohol and other drugs may indeed numb certain feelings, but "unpleasant" activities, such as working or dieting, obviously do not eliminate discomfort and must be addicting for some other reason. However, all addictions help us cope with life experiences in a different way. On some level, all addictions lock the door to our closet and keep unprocessed memories in storage.

THE PSYCHE'S CONTRIBUTION

Most people think that winning is the whole point of gambling. You know, that I go to make extra money on "the slots." The truth is that winning is just a good excuse to go. When I win, I can justify it to my friends. But I really hate winning. It gets in the way of playing. Being there is so soothing—it's like a spiritual experience. I can just get into the lights and sounds and I don't have to think about anything. When I win a jackpot, I have to stop and take care of business. I wish the world would just go away and let me play.

—Gladys S.

In daily life, we are constantly confronted with vast amounts of information at once—some important, some not. Our psyche must ignore the majority of this information and focus on the most critical data so we are not overwhelmed. This decision about where to direct our attention is relatively predictable because it is based on survival: we concentrate first on that which will keep us alive. Focusing our attention in this way is certainly a logical and beneficial approach, but it is also ripe for abuse by a psyche determined to keep past events buried. In fact, the psyche's need to prioritize life-threatening events over day-to-day issues is the key to the non-physical aspect of addiction.

In the psyche's list of priorities, there are three primary categories: crises, important current situations, and mundane ordinary events.

Crises are, of course, first to get our attention, and during a crisis, our concentration becomes very narrow. We tune out all distractions and give the situation our full consideration. In order to keep this focus, the psyche avoids the normal activities of integration, such as making connections between current data and past events, unless it encounters a particularly intense trigger. The entire crisis experience is simply stored to be dealt with later. This suspension of integration allows us to concentrate on survival and keeps distracting memories buried.

Although crises are relatively easy to define, important current situations, which are the psyche's second priority, are not quite as clear-cut. Though important situations are as effective as crises at keeping old events in storage, the determination of "important" depends to some extent on exactly how urgent we make the situation. Activities such as studying for a test, watching a television show or finishing a video game are significant for no real reason other than that we choose to give them our undivided attention. In the absence of a crisis or critical situation, however that is defined, the psyche turns its attention to its third priority: mundane current activities. It is only in this state that the psyche resumes processing events tucked safely away in storage. As a result, old issues stay on hold until life is calm and quiet.

Addictions manipulate this pecking order by convincing the psyche and us that the addiction, whatever it might be, is a crisis or important current situation. This defense keeps overwhelming events in storage as long as we focus on the addiction. While the pain and urgency of withdrawal symptoms boosts the crisis component of physical addictions, the addiction's status as a crisis or critical situation is due primarily to nothing more than the importance our psyche places on it. The tremendous thought and energy invested in an addiction—even when we are not actively engaged in the behavior or in using the substance—keeps past experiences buried. The high, rush, trance or buzz is certainly an added benefit, but the real driving force is the need to concentrate our energy toward the addiction and away from the closet.

Though the psyche's use of such a destructive coping mechanism to achieve a rather mundane end may seem odd, we must remember that the psyche views overwhelming events as incredibly dangerous. Its main concern is keeping these memories buried. However, the psyche has only two options for accomplishing this task. One alternative is sheer willpower, which drains our energy, causes depression and is often ineffective. Addictions, on the other hand, do an excellent job of keeping the past buried. In addition to being tremendously effective, they also have the advantage of giving us energy and a sense of purpose. Most importantly, many are very subtle—subtle enough, in fact, to function undetected unless we are familiar with how they operate.

The subtleties of less obvious addictions also add to their attractiveness. Since we often do not recognize these discreet addictions, they may seem like appealing options for keeping events in storage and taming our monsters. These "under the radar" addictions—such as excessive exercising, doing crafts, reading, and even, for some people, focusing on religion—are easily confused with mentally and physically healthy coping mechanisms. However, a clear understanding of how addictions work makes it easier to see the problems these inconspicuous addictions can cause. When we understand the role addictions play in helping our psyche deal with stored overwhelming life experiences, we will be able to recognize and respond appropriately even to our most thoroughly camouflaged addictions.

DISTRACTION

> My thing was commercial jingles—you know, "Sometimes, you feel like a nut... sometimes you don't." Oh, I felt like a nut all right. It was CONSTANT–the banter in my head. Non-stop, 24/7. I'd even wake up in the middle of the night with a jingle running through my mind. What I wouldn't have given for a little peace and quiet! It started on my way to school to keep from thinking about the things my mom would say to me. I'd have to clear my head so I didn't start crying in class. It worked great. But then I couldn't stop. It was awful.
>
> —Jackie M.

Addictions use a variety of tricks to keep painful memories and feelings in storage, ranging from simple distraction, as in Jackie's case, to elaborate ploys that make specific issues and feelings seem to vanish entirely. When the goal of an addiction is to merely keep our mind occupied, we usually become hooked on activities that feel good physically or psychologically. For example, we may become obsessed with television, because we enjoy the trance-like state it generates, or we may gamble on horse races, because we like the rush. Those of us who are workaholics probably enjoy the sense of importance involved in professional success. However, it is also possible to become addicted to distractions that are emotionally neutral, such as focusing on cracks in the sidewalk or commercial jingles.

While most distraction addictions are relatively simple, one of the most common and destructive is the complex addiction of codependence. The term "codependence" originally referred to the tendency seen in spouses of recovering alcoholics and drug addicts to sabotage the addicts' sobriety. As much as codependent spouses insisted that they wanted the addiction to stop, they often seemed invested in keeping the addiction alive. We now understand that codependence can operate in any context and involves the pattern of distracting ourselves from our own issues by focusing on the needs of others. Clearly, maintaining this type of distraction is easier when the other person's life is chaotic and out of control, as is the case with many alcoholics and addicts, but we can also *excessively* focus on fixing the life of someone with a mental illness, providing for the poor, or even helping stray animals.

It is easy to be caught up in the impression that distraction addictions are relatively benign. After all, our culture glorifies distraction and has made an art of staying busy—and indeed, most activities are fine when we are not using them as distractions. However, we must be able to relax and focus on our own issues in order to process information. Since distraction addictions work by maintaining a constant sense of being busy and occupied, the addictive behavior can take over our life and obliterate our sense of self. Not only are we in constant danger of being blindsided by our monsters, but we also tend to become so disconnected from our sense of self that we can end up isolated from others and detached from our own life. Worst of all, these addictions can push us into very destructive choices, such as when a codependent spouse sabotages his or her partner's sobriety.

On the other hand, distraction addictions are relatively easy to combat because they rely on the most basic defense—obsessing over a particular behavior so our psyche has no energy to process painful events. Since this type of addiction requires that we maintain a consistent focus and a constant sense of urgency, once we realize the purpose of the distracting behavior, we can simply wean ourselves from the addiction while simultaneously dealing with any issues that surface. As we decrease the problem behavior, our mind will begin to unwind and access unprocessed issues. Though this can be uncomfortable, especially at first, it is not a complicated process. Most addictions, however, are somewhat more difficult to recognize and overcome. Treating these addictions requires a more complex approach.

EXERCISE 5 - 2

Everyone uses distraction to a certain degree, but it is important to know if you have developed a serious problem in this area. Do you make sure that a television is available on vacations? Does the thought of being without your DVD or Internet service make you anxious? Would you be lost without your car radio? In your journal, make a list of the different ways you fill your life with busyness. Then, try this experiment: find a quiet place away from other people and noise, and try to be still for two or three hours. If you start feeling very nervous or are totally unable to calm your mind, you may be using distraction to keep your closet door closed. Make a note of this and discuss it with your counselor.

AVOIDANCE

I was really young when I got involved with Fred, and he was my world. Now, looking back on it, I think he wanted it that way. If I didn't call, he was on the phone wanting to know why. He promised me the world and I believed him—100%. But after we had sex, that was it. He dropped me like I had the plague. I was totally devastated. I can't tell you how shocked and hurt and ashamed I felt. I thought I'd never recover.

When I met Jack, I wasn't that impressed. He was fresh out of jail and had a drug problem, but there was something about him, like he needed me. I guess feeling needed made me feel safe. But before I knew it, I needed him—100%. I tried to leave, especially when he started getting abusive, but I could only stay away for a couple days. Then I HAD to go back. I felt like a fish out of water.

—Mary F.

Avoidance addictions, like basic distraction, help keep painful emotions buried. However, the compulsive behavior or activity involved in an avoidance addiction is intended to dodge *particular* emotions and body sensations. In other words, avoidance addictions involve specific behaviors that will keep certain feelings buried. For example, someone who experienced starvation as a child may eat constantly to avoid feeling hungry, or someone who was teased excessively for being awkward may develop a shopping addiction to keep from feeling unattractive. However, avoidance addictions are rarely this straightforward. Usually, the connection between the emotion being avoided and the addictive behavior is complicated by additional feelings and experiences.

Relationship addictions, for example, are often attempts to avoid triggering buried feelings of loneliness, grief, rejection and abandonment. Although other issues can also cause us to obsessively cling to a partner, the most common reason for insisting on being in a relationship is the need to keep old loss in the closet. Remember that feelings from a current situation will bring up similar buried feelings, creating an overwhelming combination. This means that the pain of ending an existing relationship will often unearth unprocessed abandonment and rejection from storage. For example, Mary's intense reaction to the thought of leaving her second boyfriend is actually a combination of old and current pain.

Mary's abandonment by Fred: put in storage

████████████████████████████

Mary's feelings of loss about ending relationship with Jack

███████████

Mary's hurt combines to make leaving Jack impossible

████████ + ████████████████████████

These triggered feelings of loss not only make ending a relationship difficult, but they also explain some of the "illogical" behaviors associated with relationship addictions, such as the tendency to quickly jump from one bad relationship to another. Because the euphoria of a new relationship eliminates the pain of a breakup, the psyche idealizes people we barely know and makes them seem like good partners. Fear of triggered old loss is also behind the cycle of separating and reunifying frequently seen in relationship addictions. This cycle happens because, in spite of being rationally aware that we need to leave, the painful combination of triggered old rejection and current loss overwhelms our rational self, and we go back.

While the connection between abandonment and relationship addiction is relatively apparent, some avoidance addictions suppress feelings that seem to have little to do with the behavior displayed in the addiction. Eating disorders, for example, appear on the surface to be driven simply by a fear of being overweight. In reality, however, they are more likely to be motivated by much more complex issues. For instance, an only child with over-achieving, controlling parents might grow up feeling as though she's constantly under a microscope. She could develop an eating disorder as a way to avoid feeling too visible, or to regain a sense of control in her life.

A woman with a sexual abuse history, on the other hand, may become anorexic to forestall developing sexually—to avoid "becoming a woman." Someone who was taught not to express anger under any circumstances

71

might find that an eating disorder is an effective and socially acceptable way to vent hidden anger without triggering the guilt of expressing anger directly. While those of us who are not in the grip of an eating disorder may not see the connection between obsessing about one's weight and avoiding feelings of powerlessness or memories of sexual abuse, this difficulty identifying the painful issues behind the addiction simply illustrates how effectively it does its job.

Notice that the addiction's ability to lock our feelings away also increases the likelihood that those painful emotions will compound themselves and reinforce their own consequences, in much the same way that emotional ruts and triggered thoughts do. For example, the avoidance addiction that Mary used to repress past abandonment resulted in abuse by Jack—which undoubtedly caused additional feelings of loneliness, abandonment and rejection. While this escalation pattern is particularly common with avoidance addictions, it can occur with other addictions as well. Even physical dependencies can compound buried feelings when overwhelming shame, powerlessness and depression increase the likelihood of further drug and alcohol use.

This snowball effect also creates a serious additional problem. As we might expect, the growing backlog of emotions in storage increases the likelihood that we will turn again and again to addictions to help us cope, and the strength of the addiction needed to keep things buried escalates as well. With avoidance addictions, this is particularly problematic, because over time, the psyche can create avoidance addictions that are so incredibly complex we can have serious difficulty unraveling them to find the emotions behind the avoidance. Not all addictions involve running away from problem feelings, however. Sometimes, our psyche takes the opposite approach and uses a matching addiction to hide buried memories by making up "here and now" excuses for disturbing feelings.

MATCHING

One of the hardest things I ever had to admit to myself was that I really wanted to be hit. I know it's not normal. In the shelter, I kept hearing all these women talking about how awful it was for them.

It made me feel more and more weird. I wanted to be hit. It was like something inside me was driving me to it. After Jim took that anger management class, things were so calm. I couldn't stand it. I was so tense all the time. I knew it was coming, and I wanted to get it over with. Now that I look back on it, I really drove him to it that last time.

—Peg V.

Of all possible addictions, matching addictions are among the most difficult to understand and recognize. Matching addictions serve the special purpose of helping the psyche deal with unprocessed feelings that will not stay buried. When old feelings consistently fall out of the closet, our psyche has to find a way to cope, and compulsively finding reasons that allow us to attribute old emotions to our current situation works wonders. This pattern of habitually finding a current excuse for our irrational emotions allows us to avoid acknowledging their true source. It keeps us from having to consider the "dangerous" possibility that a painful past experience is the real cause. As a result, matching addictions keep the *memory* in storage while giving us a way to cope with all the *old feelings* that insist on falling out.

On the surface, the intense feelings experienced with matching addictions seem similar to those of triggered emotions, but these are entirely different problems that should not be confused. Triggering happens when old feelings are pulled out of storage by an unavoidable current situation, whereas matching addictions involve compulsively—and on a subconscious level, purposefully—creating situations that correspond to a preexisting internal emotional state. The emotion is already present; we just generate a situation in the here and now to explain it. For example, in Peg's case, even though Jim was no longer angry, previous fights had left behind an uncomfortable residual feeling of impending conflict. Peg had to cause conflict to justify that feeling, or she would be forced to look at painful memories of previous fights.

Someone who obsessively hates is also often in the thrall of a matching addiction. Hate addictions are relatively common and are the reason for many hideous hate crimes. When we encounter people who compulsively rage against others, such as neo-Nazis, members of the KKK, or people involved in gay bashing, we may wonder why they seem so driven. As odd as it may seem, the motivation behind these crimes is often the anger itself. By creating an external scapegoat, someone who "deserves" their wrath, hate addicts find a reason for the feelings they can no longer keep in storage. Of course, the scapegoat is not the true source of their anger at all, but it allows them to justify their feelings and ignore the real cause.

Although matching addictions may seem strange, they are not uncommon. For example, children with residual abandonment—for example, those in foster care—are often hostile and seem to ask for rejection, and people with high levels of internalized guilt frequently engage in behavior that creates a reason for their shame. Sometimes, we may assume that a matching addiction gives us a chance to "express" a problem emotion. These efforts to feel and communicate the emotion seem to be progress towards resolving it, but this is far from the truth. As we will discuss in Chapter 6, we need to acknowledge the real reason(s) behind an emotion in order to heal. Matching addictions do not allow this to happen.

MIXED ADDICTIONS

> Mom was absolutely frantic by the time she died. I don't know if it was the shame that got her or the drugs. She was a stripper. She said that she liked the power she felt, but she never looked powerful when she came home. She looked like a little girl, utterly humiliated. I think it gave her a reason to feel bad about herself. But she felt bad about herself anyway, even when she wasn't dancing. And she had a lot of fear too. And dancing kept her busy. She was always doing something, her hair, her costumes. Like I said, I don't know what got her, but by the end, she was like a rat caught in a trap with no way out—absolutely frantic.
>
> —Randy G.

Sometimes, it is not easy to find the underlying reason for addictive behavior, especially when our addiction serves multiple purposes, as in the case of a mixed addiction. On some level, every addiction has many goals, but certain addictions are inherently better at multitasking. One example of an addiction that incorporates components of distraction, avoidance and matching is an obsession with crisis. This addiction usually starts during a period of extended extreme stress, such as a long-term illness, a time of severe financial difficulty, or a childhood spent in a seriously dysfunctional home. After the crisis is over, relaxing means dealing with emotions that have been ignored, so it is easier to look for and focus on another crisis. Eventually, we can become stuck in crisis mode.

While being addicted to crisis may seem counterintuitive, it is actually an incredibly effective way to keep memories in storage. Crisis is the ultimate distraction. Because our psyche focuses on crises first, this addiction is particularly good at keeping our attention off the past. Its ability to help us avoid feeling out of control also makes it an incredibly potent avoidance addiction. The constant sense of being in crisis mode—prepared for any contingency—allows us to sidestep the tremendously aversive feeling of powerlessness. Furthermore, we can use matching to cope with any feelings of upheaval that happen to leak out, because the crisis gives us an external excuse for the old feelings that fall out of

---

EXERCISE 5 - 3

Avoidance addictions are somewhat more prevalent than matching addictions, but both are relatively common. To assess your use of these defenses, go back to your list of problem emotions from Chapter 4. Ask yourself how many emotions you obsessively avoid—for example, do you avoid the vulnerability involved in meeting someone in person by having online relationships? Also, ask yourself if you set up situations that re-create your problem feelings, such as sabotaging yourself when you are about to be successful to justify feeling like a failure. Reflect on your answers to these questions in your journal.

storage. We see the current crisis in our life as the cause of those chaotic feelings, not vice versa.

Although crisis addiction is probably the clearest example of an addiction that serves many purposes, it is certainly not alone. In reality, we can use any addiction for any function. Some activities and substances will, of course, inherently perform certain functions better than others, but there are no hard and fast rules about this, or even about what can be considered addicting. Anything at all—from sex to stamp collecting, from alcohol to advertisements—has the potential to be a distraction, a means of avoidance or a way of matching exposed feelings. The biggest indication that some behavior or substance is addicting is simply that it helps our psyche keep those past overwhelming experiences in storage.

While there are no black and white rules about which purpose any specific behavior or substance can serve, knowing the way our addiction of choice works can help us target the underlying issue during recovery. An addiction to sex, for example, may be used as a simple distraction, or on the other hand, as a way to avoid loneliness. Though the addictions appear similar on the surface, we would not approach treatment in the same way. For example, in the first instance, a simple relaxation exercise would probably allow underlying memories to surface, while the latter would require gradually decreasing the fear of loneliness. In every case, however, we must remember that we are removing an important coping mechanism. We will need to make up for this loss.

OVERWHELMING EVENTS INCOGNITO

I've been on meds for most of the last 20 years, and I can't see that they've done me a bit of good. Whether I am on the stuff or not, I still have nightmares. I still get so angry I want to kill somebody. My mood swings are horrible. At first, I thought I had manic depression. It seemed to make sense, but the meds didn't help. Then my counselor suggested that it might be because of Nam. At first, I thought he was nuts, but when I thought about it, that is exactly when it started: right after I got back.

—Brad J.

Whether our particular battle is numbing, depression, tension, triggered emotions, or addictions, we all struggle with the monsters of unprocessed experiences. In addition to the devastation caused by these emotional problems, considerable additional and avoidable turmoil is created when we confuse the effects of life experiences with physiological problems. Clearly, nature and nurture produce strikingly similar emotional results. The similarity between psychic drain and biochemical depression is one example, but there are actually many instances when the symptoms of unprocessed experiences mirror those of biochemical problems, and vice versa.

As we have learned, buried events can make us see, hear, taste, smell and physically feel things that do not exist: a phenomenon that duplicates the hallucinations present with severe depression and psychotic disorders. Buried memories can also cause mood swings, anger outbursts and depressive dips, which are normally associated with Bipolar Disorder. Difficulty concentrating and spaciness occur both when the psyche is ambivalent about connecting with buried memories and in cases of Attention Deficit Hyperactivity Disorder (ADHD). Finally, triggering can cause recurrent obsessive thoughts and compulsive behaviors, which are also indicative of Obsessive Compulsive Disorder.

Fortunately, we do not need to blindly guess at the underlying reason for our symptoms. Certain red flags will tell us when our problem is due primarily to life experiences. For example, symptoms that originate immediately after a specific overwhelming event, like Brad's, are most likely connected with that experience. We should also look for problem reactions that mirror feelings or thoughts that are in storage, as with Sarah in Chapter 4, whose suicidal thoughts mimicked her desire to die while being raped. Finally, the number of stored memories in our closet is also an excellent gauge. If we know that we have many overwhelming experiences in storage, we can be relatively sure that they are contributing to our symptoms on some level.

Knowing whether our symptoms are caused by life experiences or physiological disorders tells the best treatment to address the primary cause of our symptoms—medication, psychotherapy, or both. We should be aware, however, that at times, personal biases and fears can interfere with finding the correct approach to healing. Those of us who feel threatened by either medication or psychotherapy may be tempted to ignore the real problem so we can use the less intimidating treatment. We may settle for what is comfortable, rather than what is best. However, this tactic will not work. We must be willing to look at the true reason for our issues—experiential or physiological—and use whatever approach is necessary if we hope to make any real progress.

It is also important to remember that we can deal with both biochemical issues and life experiences. As with psychic drain and biochemical depression, there is overlap. Even in cases where the primary cause of our problem is life experiences, medication can often decrease the intensity of symptoms and increase the psyche's ability to integrate memories. We still must deal with those events, but medication can help us cope, improve our functioning, and facilitate healing. On the other hand, most biochemical disorders are also compounded by the presence of buried overwhelming experiences, so it is usually helpful to also address any trauma history that may be present, regardless of our diagnosis.

TOWARD HEALING

They say that knowing the reason is half the battle, and it does keep me from feeling like it's all my fault. But I don't just want something or someone to blame. I want to get better. I want to stop doing all the crazy stuff that I do. Knowing that there is a reason for how I act helps, but it's not enough. I want to be healthy. I want to be sane again!

—Micki D.

Seeing the connection between stored overwhelming events and our emotional problems clarifies that our reactions are not as random and irrational as they may seem. Even so, this knowledge can sometimes feel like cold comfort: buried experiences still take an incredible toll on our lives, and understanding why this happens does not always prevent further damage. The monsters in our closets damage our most treasured relationships, hinder our occupational success and leave us feeling unable to manage our own emotions. Although storing the leftover pieces of unprocessed experiences was our only alternative at the time these events happened, the consequences of continuing to store and avoid them are enormous.

Fortunately, it is not necessary to continue suffering these consequences. The mechanisms of integration, avoidance and storage can be more than the reflexive responses of our psyche. We can also learn to use them consciously and purposefully to deal with overwhelming experiences, both when events happen and even long after they are over. When we understand how different therapy techniques interact with these functions of the psyche, we can minimize the damage caused by current painful experiences and heal our oldest wounds. With the right know-how, we can work with integration, storage and avoidance to not only keep future events from affecting us but also to conquer the monsters already stored in our psyche's closet.

Chapter Six

INTEGRATION: THE ORIGINAL CLOSET CLEANER

Progress, man's distinctive mark alone
Not God's, not the beasts'
God is, they are
Man partly is and wholly hopes to be

—Robert Browning

ealing is a multifaceted process. Depending on our particular needs, it might include integrating unprocessed experiences, using storage and avoidance more effectively, or developing healthier coping skills to change how we interact with the world. Sometimes, we can undertake these tasks on our own—for example, by writing about difficult experiences, reading self-help books, or talking with siblings about past traumas and family dynamics. Trying to inte grate experiences on our own can be positive and productive, especially when we are working to keep current ordeals from going into storage. However, in most cases, recovery from painful events, particularly traumatic past experiences, requires the focused assistance available in psychotherapy.

Psychotherapy is, at its core, a directed approach to healing the symptoms of overwhelming events, but the specifics of this process have in the past been difficult to decipher. Historically, there have been surprising levels of animosity between the various approaches to therapy, which has made it difficult to grasp the bigger picture of emotional problems. These same turf wars have also obscured our ability to see the general patterns of recovery. As a result, it was easy to find very specific information about different forms of treatment, but information about the process of treatment itself was almost impossible to locate. Until now, we were given discourses on the various trees living in the forest of recovery, rather than a map to guide us through the woods. Although information about different therapies may be interesting, a general understanding of how we heal and how to facilitate this process is much more beneficial for those of us actually needing counseling.

Fortunately, understanding the mechanisms underlying all forms of therapy is much easier than it may seem, because therapies share a common foundation in the functions of the human psyche. In other words, every approach to therapy must use integration, storage and/or avoidance. Any treatment that helps us deal with the symptoms discussed in the first half of this book has to rely on these three mechanisms. The differences between the various approaches lie not so much in what they try to accomplish but in how they achieve their goals. This bears repeating. In spite of the many apparent differences between the various approaches, the only true distinction is in how they activate the psyche's functions.

Normally, we would look at the techniques used by various therapies to understand how the therapeutic process operates, but there are hundreds of these different techniques, with new ones being developed every day. A more effective way to look at the dynamics behind this process is to explore the mechanisms accessed by these techniques. In other words, just as every approach shares the foundation of working with the three functions of the psyche, so must every single technique used by every therapy use the same mechanisms—the various pieces of who we are—to access these functions. Therapeutic techniques must work with the different aspects of who we are as a person, as a human.

Regardless of which technique we employ, we will find that we must use our emotions, thoughts, behaviors, capacity for insight, subconscious abilities and innate physiological responses to integrate, store or avoid life experiences. While we may not be accustomed to thinking of our "self" as functional in this way, we work with these pieces all the time. In everyday life, for example, we cry to integrate grief, or use our imagination to create make-believe lovers or friends to avoid loneliness. In psychotherapy, however, these pieces of our selves are used consciously and for the greatest impact.

THE PSYCHE'S TOOLS

> *When I first started therapy, I knew I needed help, but I didn't have a clue why I was there. It was really scary. The first time I met my therapist, I didn't even know what questions to ask. It was like I was shooting in the dark. Recovery just seemed like a giant mystery that I had to take on faith. I got through it, and I'm glad I went, but I wish I understood a little more about it.*
>
> *—Cheri F.*

We have learned that the psyche has three options for dealing with events: integration, storage and avoidance. Regardless of whether the psyche is tackling events on its own or with our conscious help and guidance, these three functions are the only alternatives at its disposal. However, we will need tools to accomplish these psychological tasks, just as we need tools to carry out tasks in other contexts. For example, imagine that instead of personal growth, we have a goal of repairing a run-down house. In order to achieve this goal, we would need to complete the tasks of pounding, turning, and pulling various screws, bolts, boards and whatnots, and we will have a variety of tools available for these tasks: hammers, screwdrivers, crowbars, and so on.

Similarly, to achieve the goal of rebuilding our psyche, we will need to integrate, store and avoid a variety of events and issues, and we have a well-stocked toolbox at our disposal. Our emotions, thoughts, behaviors, capacity for insight, subconscious abilities and innate physiological responses are these tools. If we know how these aspects of our "self" work, they can accomplish amazing feats: integrating the most painful event, shoring up our storage abilities, and moving us away from the closet and back into our life. When wielded by skilled hands for the greatest effect possible, they can conquer both the overwhelming experiences that happen day to day and those that have already been put in storage.

To use these tools most effectively, however, we first need to learn how they function. No one would take on the job of renovating a run-down house without a basic knowledge of all the necessary tools. We would certainly not undermine our efforts by focusing only on a hammer and screwdriver, ignoring all our other options. In our emotional recovery, the different parts of ourselves can accomplish a wide variety of jobs. While we will inevitably feel more comfortable working with certain aspects of our selves, we should be at least moderately familiar with all our options, including how to combine tools to accomplish the most difficult tasks.

In the next few chapters, we will discuss how to use the pieces of who we are to integrate, store and avoid unprocessed experiences. For those already in therapy, this map of the overall process may make it easier to resolve past experiences more effectively. (Remember, however, that we should unearth past events only with the guidance of a trained therapist.) Those of us considering treatment in the future will also have a chance to look at the way the various options work, so we can find those that best fit our concerns, needs and personality. Most importantly, a map of the healing process will help us all know how to deal with future overwhelming experiences, so we have a chance to keep new monsters from taking up residence in our closet.

INTEGRATION'S SABOTEUR

My doctor told me to go to a counselor, because he couldn't do anything for the strange feeling I had in my throat. Boy, did I resent the implication that it was "all in my head," but I was desperate, so I went. That's when I realized that it started after Bob forced me to perform oral sex. It was so awful I just blocked it out. But I guess my mind couldn't keep it buried. I just kept feeling it in my throat over and over without knowing where it was coming from.

—Tina B.

Of the psyche's three tasks, integration is undoubtedly the most helpful in the healing process. Finishing integration allows us to totally resolve any destructive emotions and reactions that cling to an experience. In other words, completing any integration that our mind cannot finish on its own eliminates the negative qualities connected with that overwhelming event. Remember that regardless of how awful an experience was, once our psyche is able to integrate it, either on its own or with our help, the event will not have a negative effect on our feelings and reactions. This means that integration does away with the need for other treatment, with the possible exception of therapy to address the issues of daily life, such as developing coping skills, building a support system, etc.

Many of us will find, therefore, that integration is our treatment of choice; the trick is finding the best tool to complete this particular task. Although we can sometimes use our thoughts or imagination to complete integration, the most effective tool for this job is our emotions. The reason emotions are so essential to integration is that they are usually the reason why processing becomes blocked in the first place. Though, as mentioned earlier, the exact reason this happens is still not entirely clear, the disturbing qualities of certain emotions undoubtedly are a primary cause, because emotions are the most intensely disturbing aspects of an event. In fact, aside from certain body sensations, for example, the pain of a first-degree burn or extremely loud noises, emotions are the only truly upsetting part of an event.

This idea may seem counterintuitive. We are used to thinking of thoughts and images as distressing on their own—but in reality, these components become upsetting only when combined with our emotions. Images are only snapshots, and thoughts are just words. They rely on emotions to give them value and make them troubling. Emotions, on the other hand, can be disturbing on their own, and thus are the piece of an overwhelming experience that interferes with integration. Natural processing, therefore, is clogged by emotions that are too intense for the psyche to digest. By processing those feelings, we process the event as well. Put simply, we use our feelings to integrate the event.

EXERCISE 6 - 1

To illustrate the impact of emotions on processing, think about two or three of the events listed in your journal and guess the reason they were not processed. Chances are that your psyche was unable to process them due to very intense feelings. If, on the other hand, you cannot identify any disturbing feelings connected with these events, you may want to explore the possibility that you are avoiding feeling painful emotions.

EXPRESSION

> *The flashbacks happen all the time, especially when I try to sleep.*
> *They scare the crap out of me. I feel like it's happening again. I*
> *know it happened over ten years ago, but it still seems like right*
> *now. The feelings are so terrifying. I don't know if I can deal with*
> *them, but on the other hand, if facing them head on makes them go*
> *away, it's worth it.*
>
> —*Rachel B.*

Since intense emotions are usually the roadblock to natural integration, we need to resolve those emotions to finish integrating the event in question. However, facing overwhelming feelings, especially when they have been locked deep in storage, is no minor task. The psyche is so motivated to keep old feelings buried that it may use the defenses of blinding us to the existence of these feelings or convincing us that repressing them is keeping us sane. It will often maintain that purposely dredging up the past is pointless and counterproductive. The argument in favor of ignoring painful old emotions is compelling—so much so that even some scientists subscribe to it. There are researchers who say that focusing on "negative" emotions encourages the psyche to hold onto them (Geen and Quanty, 1977; Tavris, 1982).

However, research on the expression of feelings has rarely distinguished between routine and overwhelming feelings, and it has ignored the critical steps necessary for achieving emotional closure. These are serious oversights. As we have seen, the mind processes ordinary and overwhelming emotions in very different ways. While paying little attention to normal emotions is healthy and appropriate, overwhelming feelings require a particular process. Assessing the effectiveness of expressing overwhelming emotions without looking at this process makes as much sense as researching the concept of baking without using recipes.

ELUSIVE INGREDIENTS

The anger just seemed so out of control for so long. I felt like there was absolutely nothing I could do to make it stop. And the idea that I needed to express it seemed so crazy. That was all I was doing. I was yelling and screaming constantly. But when I got angry at my dad in therapy, that was different. I couldn't believe how changed I felt, like two tons had been lifted off my shoulders. Now I know what "closure" means.

—Bob P.

Although we undoubtedly expect to have an instinctive knowledge of how to handle emotions, unleashing overwhelming emotions is more complex and psychologically threatening than expressing their everyday counterparts. As a result, the psyche is often compelled to sabotage the expression process. Unfortunately, all the psyche needs to do to put a kink in the works is to delete one of expression's three necessary ingredients. These three critical ingredients are: 1) experiencing the emotion in our body, 2) focusing on the true cause of that feeling, and 3) direct venting. Although some of the new therapies discussed in Chapter 9 may be able to resolve emotions without these three components, integrating an overwhelming experience—either something from our closet or a current disturbing situation—through the use of feelings usually requires these three steps.

While we might expect that it would be easy to include all three elements, it's a task easier said than done. For example, feeling the emotion in our body can be much trickier than it sounds. Far too often we settle for intellectual awareness—"I know that I must be feeling angry"—rather than actually experiencing the emotion on a physical level: tightness in the stomach, heart pounding, tension in our shoulders, etc. Even emotions that are triggered frequently can suddenly become amazingly slippery during venting. Rather than experiencing the physical sensations, we may become remarkably numb and detached. This roadblock to the expression process is minor, however, compared with the challenges of identifying the true cause and venting effectively.

THE SOURCE

> *For years, I thought my girlfriend was making me unhappy. We just weren't getting along. We yelled at each other all the time. I kept thinking I should leave, but I felt guilty when I did. After five years, I finally did, and I still wasn't happy. I thought about our arguments all the time. I was reliving them, over and over, like I wanted to get in one last word that would prove I was right and she was wrong.*
>
> *I was so angry and unhappy and frustrated. I thought she had ruined my life. Imagine my surprise when I realized I had been unhappy even before I met her—that it all started when my brother used to beat me up. It turned out that my girlfriend wasn't why I had been unhappy after all. It had nothing to do with her!*
>
> *—James L.*

When integrating events through emotions, it is critical to identify the real source of our feeling. This may seem easy enough, especially when we plan to vent about a particular past event or an overwhelming current situation. However, even if we think we know the real cause of our feelings, we need to consider the possibility that our emotions, like James', stem from an earlier buried experience. Remember that feelings from the past will often come up during later events. The intense trig-gered feelings are easily confused with a genuine reaction to the current situation. We must be sure we have identified the true, not just the appar-ent, cause.

It is amazingly easy to believe that our feelings are due to here-and-now problems, even when the real source is in our closet. For example, in Chapter Four we met John, who blew up over not finding his socks. If John were venting his anger, he might focus on his disorganized wife, who never puts his socks away, or on his boss, who makes him work so much he cannot keep his house in order. In either case, he would be miss-ing the mark, because John's anger is actually much older than his current situation. Although in most cases this is just a simple mistake, at times, this tendency to blame the here-and-now grows into a full-blown defense. This ability to avoid expressing and resolving old feelings by reflexively blaming a current issue or person is particularly insidious, but it is certainly not our psyche's only option for hiding the true reason for our feelings.

Besides using the defense of focusing on the present, our psyche can also conceal the real cause by arguing that we have always felt the identified emotion. With this defense, the psyche convinces us that there is no event that originally generated this feeling—it is, and always has been, an innate part of who we are. This defense works because we will not dig around for the cause of an emotion that has no identifiable external origin. However, we should not be fooled. In spite of how it may seem, our pain does have a definite source. Just as our entire finger can hurt from a sliver that is located in one tiny spot, emo-tions that seem to come from everywhere actually have a very specific origin.

In spite of the additional challenges presented by the psyche's defenses, finding the real source of an emotion is not a complicated process once we know where and how to look. The first step is to iden-tify when the problem feeling initially became an ongoing part of our life. Since problem emotions come up repeatedly after they are imbed-ded in our psyche by an overwhelming event, looking for when we did not experience an emotion on a regular basis can help us find its origin. We need to poke around in our memory bank to trace it back to its painful source, as we would if we were looking for that sliver in our finger.

Another option is to look at the nuances of the emotion for clues about the source experience. Remember that when an experience goes into storage, it takes with it all the emotional details that were part of the original overwhelming event. For example, John did not just feel angry about not finding his socks. John felt the anger of a powerless, out-of-control six-year-old child. Joan did not just feel abandoned by her boyfriend in the restaurant. She felt like a little girl who had lost the person she loved most in the whole world. These nuances, particularly the sense of our age, can tell us a great deal about that original source event.

Nuances are also the best way to determine whether or not we have identified the correct source of an emotion. While the nuances will not make complete sense in later contexts when the feeling is triggered—think of Joan in the restaurant—they will be a perfect fit with the original source event. If they do not match the event we are working on, we should keep looking. Sometimes, identifying source experiences requires that we explore the possibility that later overwhelming events compounded feelings left behind from the original source. For example, if Joan still feels plagued by residual abandonment after working on the loss of her father, she should look at her subsequent experiences with her stepfather to see if those experiences added to her stored feelings. In most

---

EXERCISE 6 - 2

To practice identifying a source, think about the list of problem emotions in your journal. Pick one of the most troubling emotions and work with your counselor to follow it back to its origin. Try to identify a time when this emotion first entered your life, and examine the nuances of the emotion to see if they match the feelings you had during an overwhelming event at that time. If that feeling has bothered you as long as you can remember, or if it seems connected to an experience that you dissociated, see the next section.

---

cases, however, we will simply need to find an earlier event. Even if we must go back to first grade or earlier, we will usually be able to remember when a problem emotion became part of our daily life. Occasionally, however, the emotion's source really is inaccessible, which means resolving those feelings using a different approach.

FORGOTTEN SOURCE EXPERIENCES

I know I was sexually abused. I don't know how I know, I just know. It's something I've always felt, but without memories, I have no proof. And it's really affecting my life. My husband is totally frustrated with my attitude about sex. I feel awful about my body. I can't sleep. I just want to get the memories out so I can deal with them. Maybe, I should get hypnotized.

—Shirley C.

Occasionally, we are genuinely unable to remember an experience that seems to be at the root of the emotions we want to express. This difficulty remembering an event can occur due to a head injury, because the experience was extremely traumatic, or because it happened very early in our life—usually prior to age 3 or 4. Even without specific memories, however, we may feel convinced that the particular event happened. This conviction may be due to clear symptoms that indicate a certain type of trauma, or because a family member told us it happened, or simply due to a gut feeling that a specific issue caused our problem emotions or behaviors.

A common dilemma in this situation is whether or not we should invest the time and energy necessary to bring up these buried memories. Like Shirley, we may be considering hypnosis. However, pushing a memory that is truly repressed into consciousness is not advisable. As we have learned, our psyche is incredibly threatened by even the most basic non-integrated memories. If it adamantly refuses to so much as acknowledge the existence of a particular event, we can be sure that the danger of this memory is exponentially greater. Although we may be tempted to try to force our way past the defense of dissociation and access these repressed memories, this is often counterproductive and can cause us to become seriously overwhelmed.

We must remember that every defense serves a purpose. Sometimes, the psyche is terrified of the feelings connected with the repressed memory, but more often, it blocks memories to try to minimize how much is being digested at one time—limiting how many non-integrated memories are accessible. Like a good parent, the psyche refuses to let us reach for "seconds" when we have not cleaned our plate of the issues we already remember. The best approach to healing, therefore, is to focus first on the disturbing events we already can recall, even if they don't seem to be causing our most troubling symptoms. Once these events are processed and are no longer draining our energy, the psyche will usually allow repressed issues to surface. Processing the items on our plate, however, requires the final component of the expression process: direct, involved venting.

"DIRECT" AND "INVOLVED"

Saying how you feel is hard, you know? It's not that you can't express your feelings. It's just hard to talk about it. You can say that someone gets on your nerves, but writing a letter, even one you're not going to send...it's not so easy. You feel so uncomfortable. It's just awkward. It doesn't feel right.

—Cheryl G.

In some minor cases, simply knowing the reason for our feelings can bring closure, but as those with long-burning anger or anxiety from childhood abuse can testify, closure usually requires one final step. Once we are able to physically feel the emotion in our body and know its source, most of us will have to complete integration by venting—a task that is, again, much more difficult than it seems on the surface. With venting, the challenge is to make it involved and direct. In other words, we must take responsibility for our feelings and say them plainly. Though it seems simple enough, this is an undertaking that is incredibly threatening and can once more trigger the misguided good intentions of the psyche's defenses.

92

One common way the psyche shuts down venting is by convincing us that expression works only if we confront the person responsible for our injury. With this defense, the psyche tells us that unless we have been heard and validated by whomever is to blame, we have accomplished nothing. The problem with this line of reasoning is that it can be incredibly emotionally dangerous. Confronting a childhood perpetrator prior to working through our feelings leaves us tremendously emotionally vulnerable. With a huge backlog of old emotions, feelings of childhood powerlessness can easily be triggered, which puts us at a distinct disadvantage and the perpetrator in a position of control.

Fortunately, the psyche usually turns to this defense only when speaking to that person is not an option. However, the conviction that we need to be heard and validated is still able to keep us stuck, spinning our wheels and unable to heal. In reality, the perpetrator's response is not important. The primary factor allowing us to achieve closure is that we acknowledge, validate and state our feelings. This is the goal of venting, and it is this ability to express ourselves that provides emotional closure. Confrontation, on the other hand, is intended to facilitate communication with another person. While there may be times when this step will be necessary, it is better in those cases to vent beforehand. We will be more rational, calm, and focused after venting our pent-up feelings.

We also need to remember that even without the possibility of confrontation, old buried emotions can be extremely risky. Although venting about a current situation is usually safe, expressing feelings from past experiences can easily cause a serious psychological backlash. The following suggestions for venting are intended to explain the expression process so that we can take an active role in our healing and integrate current situations more easily. We SHOULD NOT attempt these activities on emotions from past experiences without the explicit support of our counselor.

THE PROCESS OF VENTING

Feeling guilty for my brother's drowning was easy. It didn't require much effort at all, and it gave me a great excuse for drinking and being self-destructive. You'd expect that telling Bobbie

93

and my parents that I was sorry for not believing he was really drowning would have been just as easy. But God, that was like pulling teeth. And even though they were there just in my imagination, I couldn't get it out.

—Scott B.

Venting emotions is a relatively simple, if at times a somewhat awkward, process. First, we will need to have a sense of the other person's presence. This is easiest if we picture him or her either in the room with us, in a scene from our past or in a setting that makes us feel safe, such as with the offending party locked in a jail cell. Once we have a sense of that person's presence, we can say how we feel out loud, yell, pound a pillow, write a letter, or even draw a picture expressing our feelings. There are many different ways to imagine the individual's presence and to express our emotions, but no matter how we choose to accomplish this task, we need to express ourselves directly.

Direct expression is not always easy. Often, we avoid owning the feeling. We may say that the other person "makes us feel" a certain way, or focus only on them and not on ourselves—for example, "you are so..."—but in order to achieve closure, we must admit how we feel directly. It is much easier to attribute our feelings and reactions to others than to call them our own, but when we vent, we must be perfectly clear who is speaking, what we are feeling and why we are feeling that way. Fortunately, there are several formats that can be used to guide us while we become accustomed to and comfortable with the expression process.

One such formula is the classic "I statement." An "I statement" involves expressing feelings using the formula "I feel _____ when you _____." For example: "I feel furious when you call me a slut" or "I feel guilty when you complain about our finances." Although this formula is extremely straightforward and effective, it may seem a little stilted and unnecessarily tame for expressing intense emotions, especially overwhelming anger. Saying "I feel furious when you _____" to express blinding rage can seem absurd. Fortunately, this is not the only way to effectively vent feelings. Another pattern is "I __[emotion]__ for __[reason]__." For example: "I hate you for hitting my mother."

94

Of course, there are many other options for expressing our feelings. We often have to try several before we find one that fits our particular needs and issues. For example, we may find that expressing childhood anger with crayons on large pieces of paper or with chalk on a chalkboard feels most comfortable. Or venting anger at an ex-spouse may be most effective if we scream at the top of our lungs and hit a chair with a child's plastic bat. We just need to be sure that we say directly how we feel and take responsibility for that feeling. However, even when we use these techniques with the help of a counselor, there are times when expression can still be sabotaged.

EXPRESSION FAILURES

> *I can't seem to get rid of all that hurt. I've done a little work on it, written a letter to Jack saying good-bye. But it hurts. I wish there was an easy way to just make the pain go away. Yes, I want to get over his death, but this doesn't seem to be working.*
>
> *—Lillian G.*

Even though expression is often difficult and painful, emotional closure—that wonderful sense that we have totally released a painful feeling—is worth the struggle. While learning to effectively avoid or contain old feelings can also be empowering, these options pale in comparison to the immense relief of completely resolving a traumatic memory. However, expression can also be time-consuming, and certain feelings—especially, for example, anxiety—may be difficult to integrate. If we do not seem to be making progress, we should check with our counselor. In most cases, we simply need to give ourselves more time. Occasionally, however, the process of expression becomes genuinely stuck, and we must look for the missing ingredients.

Of all the possibilities, the most likely culprit is an overlooked source event. Often, we have simply missed an earlier related experience or a subsequent event that compounded the feeling and therefore needs to be processed as well. There is also the possibility that one of the other components of expression is the problem. We need to ask ourselves if we are either avoiding experiencing the feelings in our body or sidestepping direct expression. As simple oversights, these glitches in the expression process are easy to resolve, but at times, they can become so reflexive and habitual that we have trouble reversing them. Our psyche can turn to them as defenses, tenaciously clinging to them to stop expression.

The psyche's avoidance of expression is notoriously inventive. Although expressing feelings is the most effective way to remove the residual feelings that block the natural integration process, the psyche is incredibly threatened by this process and will attempt to sabotage it any way it can. Unfortunately, the psyche does not always stop at simply sidestepping one or more of the three ingredients. Occasionally, when buried feelings are especially threatening, it can take drastic measures to sabotage processing by using two particularly elaborate defenses. These drastic forms of sabotage are the psyche's most creative tactics: the mutating and misdirecting of our feelings.

Chapter Seven

MUTATED AND MISDIRECTED EMOTIONS

E motions are the tool of choice for completing the integration of both past and current experiences. As long as our psyche's defenses do not interfere, emotional expression is tremendously successful at unblocking integration and thus resolving residual emotions from painful overwhelming events. However, far too often the psyche does indeed sabotage processing. Usually, this sabotage involves misplacing one of the three ingredients of expression, but the psyche may also use the powerful defenses of mutating and misdirecting emotions.

Mutation sabotages expression by changing the very nature of the emotion itself—for example, by turning anger into depression. *Misdirection* involves consistently identifying an incorrect target, such as being angry with ourselves instead of a perpetrator for childhood abuse. In both cases, we manage to avoid one of the three ingredients of expression, but in a way that is so subtle it is incredibly difficult to realize that we are actually sidestepping the real issue. On the surface, it appears that we are venting correctly. We identify a source, feel the emotion in our body, and vent—but in reality, the fictitious ingredient keeps us miles away from any real expression. With this sleight of hand, the psyche convinces us that we are dealing with our feelings while protecting us from the "threat" of real expression.

Sometimes, low processors turn to mutation and misdirection to avoid opening up their overstocked closets, for fear that an open door will bring everything tumbling out. More often, these defenses help us cope with particularly dangerous feelings, such as intense despair or anger at a violent perpetrator. Connecting with these painful feelings or their real cause can be threatening, so the psyche does what it can to evade the issue by substituting something less dangerous. In the process, however, it also shuts down integration, and worse, we often have no clue that we are not in touch with genuine issues. These defenses are so effective at masquerading as the real thing that we can spend a lifetime believing we are expressing our feelings without ever achieving closure.

LAST-DITCH DEFENSES

My counselor keeps telling me that I need to let myself feel angry with my brother for raping me and letting his friends rape me, but it's not that simple. How can you feel angry when you don't think you should be angry? That's just not how I feel, so why push it? I thought that having sex with them was just the price for hanging around my brother and his friends. If it's anybody's fault, it's mine. I should have known better. Why should I be mad at him?

— Sami C.

In the vast majority of cases, mutation and misdirection initially appear during a time of extreme stress, when the psyche is desperate to protect itself. However, these defenses do not disappear once the event is over. Since a similar feeling in a current situation will trigger the threatening feeling from the past, our psyche must continue to use the defense habitually to avoid connecting with that problem emotion in the present. For example, a very young girl being sexually abused would most likely feel angry and powerless. Expressing her anger would not be an option, so she might learn to turn the anger back on herself—misdirecting it—with self-mutilation. Even after the sexual abuse stops, any time she feels angry and powerless, she would most likely turn to self-mutilation to avoid these feelings.

Breaking the habit of mutating or misdirecting emotions is challenging and requires a two-pronged approach. The first step is to stop using these defenses in everyday life. We have to overcome our pattern of avoidance by consciously searching for the real feeling or source. Then, we must identify and deal with the underlying reason we turned to mutation or misdirection in the first place. If these defenses are simply a way to cope with being overwhelmed by too many stored events, cleaning out or re-organizing our closet may be all that is necessary. However, if we started using these defenses due to a traumatic experience, we will need to face the terrifying feelings and memories involved. In either case, dismantling these defenses requires that we be familiar with their ins and outs.

MUTATION

It's not that I don't like feeling afraid or vulnerable. It's just that I can't feel that way. It took me years, decades really, to realize that

every time I felt afraid, I would get angry. It wasn't until my
counselor pointed it out that I saw the pattern. Every time I feel
afraid – bam–no, I don't. I'm angry. Fear–bam–anger. It's magic!
—*Dave L.*

Changing the very nature of a feeling, which is the mechanism used in mutation, may seem like quite a stunt, but it is not nearly as hard as it appears, because emotions are not really the accurate representations of reality that we believe them to be. We frequently make the mistake of taking our feelings at face value. If we are angry or depressed in a particular situation, we usually assume there is something about the situation that is infuriating or disheartening. However, emotions are not concrete and static. They are shape-shifters, capable of transforming themselves to find a path around our fears. For example, anger can easily change into depression or depression into anger, shifting away from the feeling our psyche sees as most threatening.

Since these shifts between feelings follow consistent patterns, and we become accustomed to our new emotional state—feeling anger or self-loathing, for example, at the slightest provocation—it is easy to be fooled into thinking that these fictitious feelings are valid reactions. We learn to expect our new emotions and become extremely creative in finding ways to justify their presence. Regardless of how little sense the phony feelings make on a rational level, we find excuses for them. For example, before Dave realized what he was doing, he probably had dozens of justifications for feeling angry rather than vulnerable. He might have said that he hated how people treated him, or that it was infuriating not to have the security he deserved, when in reality he was just turning the energy of his fear into anger.

Friends and family also help maintain this fiction by reinforcing and encouraging our mutated emotions. Like Ellen in Chapter Four, who learned from her mother how to shut down sadness, we are taught transformations from those closest to us, and we are naturally drawn to people who are uncomfortable with the same emotions that we ourselves find distressing. As a result, we are inevitably surrounded by people who have emotional patterns similar to our own. This support for our mutation patterns, in turn, blinds us to just how inaccurate and counterproductive they are. If everyone we know cries and becomes lethargic when they are "angry," this reaction will seem normal, rather than inconsistent. The lack of support for making changes also reinforces mutation. Since those around us will discourage us from expressing feelings that they consider inappropriate, regardless of how healthy the feelings actually are, the chances that we will alter these counterproductive patterns is slim.

Sometimes, we share the defense of mutation not just with our family but with an entire culture. For example, cultural messages often give women the impression that it is not okay to be angry, or scold men for expressing "weak" emotions like grief and vulnerability. Perhaps we were raised with the idea that children who are upset with adults, no matter how they express their anger, are being "disrespectful." Feeling anger toward someone who is dead, especially a parent, is another common cultural taboo; and in some religious groups, fear, powerlessness and vulnerability are seen as a sign of lack of faith and are thus viewed as unacceptable.

Although mutation may be rooted in familial and cultural taboos, we may also learn to avoid and transform certain emotions during overwhelming experiences. As we know, these experiences leave indelible impressions on our belief systems, especially on our beliefs about emotions. Like thoughts about self-worth, the idea that certain emotions are "wrong" can become tenaciously persistent after being imprinted by an overwhelming experience. For example, if we had a parent who was cold and rejecting whenever we expressed fear, we can develop a reflexive belief that fear leads to rejection. Even the common parental rebuke, "Stop crying or I'll give you something to cry about," when administered in a painful setting, can cause us to habitually avoid sadness and tears.

Every emotion, regardless of how "unacceptable" expressing it may be, is part of our physical programming. The human body is designed to respond with sadness when faced with a serious loss, anger when annoyed, and fear or anger when threatened. We have the innate drive to respond when provoked, in the same way that we will jump when suddenly startled, or feel pain when injured. The energy connected with these emotional reactions cannot simply disappear even when acknowledging these reactions could cost us our life. We can, however, replace the problem emotion with one that seems more acceptable by changing the form the dangerous emotion's energy takes—mutating the emotional charge.

INDICATORS OF MUTATION

My son Mark has a problem with guilt. Guilt works backwards for him. When most kids feel guilty about something, they don't do it, but with Mark, it's just the opposite. When he feels guilty, he not only does it, but he gets mad about it too, like you made him do it. If I hadn't seen it a million times, I wouldn't believe it. It's so backwards, but that's how he operates.

—Sandi M.

When properly hidden from view, mutation does an amazing job of protecting us from feelings that the psyche finds threatening. However, once we know the signs that a feeling has mutated, this defense mechanism is surprisingly easy to recognize. The first clue that an emotion has been transformed is usually an ineffective venting process. If we are certain that we have taken the proper steps to vent, and the feeling does not diminish, we should ask ourselves if we are sidestepping a more suitable emotion. In other words, we need to look at the source event to see if there may be other emotions involved that we find threatening.

Fortunately, the real emotional content of an unprocessed experience is not as difficult to identify as it may seem. Since we routinely avoid emotions that our psyche believes are dangerous, we can usually identify problem emotions by simply assessing our ability to access the primary unpleasant feelings. These emotions are fear, anger, sadness, shame/guilt, powerlessness/being out of control, vulnerability and loneliness/abandonment. We should look for times when we experienced these feelings in our daily life. If we are unable to find any instances of a particular emotion, chances are our psyche considers it particularly threatening.

Sometimes, reversing our mutation patterns is also easier if we identify the feelings that are used to replace those we find frightening. To identify these substitute feelings, we need to find reactions that do not seem to belong in the context of how we view the experience. In other words, a mutated emotion does not match what bothers us about the incident. Are we feeling angry about things that others would find frightening, or guilty when most people would be afraid? Notice that this does not mean that the emotion is *out of proportion,* as in the case of triggering, but that it is *out of context.* To determine whether an emotion does not match the context, we need to identify the aspect of the event that troubles us and compare it with our feeling.

Depending on where we focus, we can have a variety of different appropriate reactions to any situation. For example, if we are dealing with having been fired and we think about how unfairly we were treated, it would be appropriate to feel angry, hurt or powerless. We may feel fear if we think about our financial predicament, or grief when we contemplate the loss of our career or coworkers. An out-of-context—or mutated—reaction would be to feel angry when thinking about a scary financial situation or afraid when thinking about how much we will miss cherished coworkers. Our reaction needs to be consistent with the particular facet of the issue we find disturbing.

On the other hand, it is not uncommon to have difficulty recognizing when our reactions do not match the context, because the psyche often rationalizes mutated feelings with habitual justifications that we come to view as logical. This means that we will most likely need the help of a trained counselor in order to recognize what is *true* as opposed to what is simply *familiar.* Understanding the common patterns in how we typically transform our feelings—which emotions tend to be avoided and which tend to be used in their place—is another invaluable asset in our quest to spot and address mutated emotions. Although all emotions are vulnerable to being altered, some are more likely to elicit an avoidance response, and others are more likely to seem "safe."

EXERCISE 7 - 1

When working on integrating experiences through feelings, you should consider whether or not you are experiencing the full range of emotions. In your journal, write a list of basic distressing emotions: fear, anger, sadness, shame/guilt, powerlessness/being out of control, vulnerability and loneliness/abandonment. Next to each of these, list a couple of incidents in which you experienced the feeling, and record how your body felt (for example, heart pounding, upset stomach, tension in the jaw, heaviness around the eyes, etc.). Also, consider the possibility that your comfort with an emotion depends on the situation. For example, you may be able to feel angry with your father but not your mother. Make a note of any feelings you tend to avoid.

CONFUSION ABOUT CONFUSION

I'm so confused about why Jack treated me like he did. If he would just tell me why, I think I could get over it. I know it sounds stupid for me to be so upset about him having other women, since he was with someone when we got involved. But I don't understand why he lied to me. Couldn't he have just told me the truth? I've tried talking to him, but he won't tell me why he did it, why he treated me that way. I know I could get over him. I just need some answers.

—Yvonne M.

Any feeling—no matter how legitimate it may be in certain circumstances—can also be used to hold the energy of other, more threatening, emotions. For example, confusion, in itself, is a valid response to a substantial influx of new information or a dramatic shift in reality, but it is also one of the best replacements for other feelings. Confusion is particularly effective at holding the energy of other feelings—in part, because it takes us from the emotional realm to the intellectual. We also cling to confusion more vigorously than to other replacement emotions, because the need to understand seems so reasonable. While we may be willing to explore the idea that our anger, guilt and depression are stand-ins for more threatening emotions, we often have trouble accepting the idea that our intense desire for an explanation is merely a way to avoid our feelings. Like Yvonne, we believe that answers will bring emotional closure.

Although our desire for an explanation seems logical on the surface, answers help only when confusion is not a mutation of other feelings. A genuine need to understand is satisfied by a logical explanation, but uncertainties that are drawing their energy from other emotions will never feel settled. We will keep asking "why" regardless of how many answers we are given. We cannot let go of our confusion because we need it to take the place of our real feelings. This difficulty accepting an explanation—along with an inability to deal with other feelings about the situation—is the best indicator that we are avoiding these other emotions.

The key to resolving mutated confusion—as well as most other trans-formed emotions—is to recognize the transformation and then deal with any feelings we are avoiding. We must ask ourselves what other emotions might fit that experience. Anger? Hurt? Fear? Sometimes, we cannot seem to find other emotions that might be involved. If this is the case, we should ask ourselves how other people might have reacted in our situation. If we can think of anything that logically seems to fit, we should explore the possibility that it applies to us as well. Once we have had a chance to acknowledge and resolve the real underlying emotions, "why" often becomes suddenly less important.

ANGER

> Living with Mom and Dad is no picnic. They are constantly put-ting me down, telling me that nothing I do is right. Maybe they're right. Maybe I am a failure. I feel like such a loser. Dad constant-ly tells me what to do, which wouldn't be so bad except he always changes it. No matter what I do, I didn't do it right. I swear he

changes the way I'm supposed to do things just so he can yell at
me. Why do I live with them anyway? I'm such a failure. Why
can't I stand on my own two feet?

—*Janine S.*

Now that we have seen an example of simple mutation, let's look at an emotion that generates a much more complicated response from the psyche: anger. Anger is an excellent example of an emotion that ends up on both sides of mutation—either as a replacement for other feelings or as the feeling we find intimidating. For some, anger does a great job of transforming "weaker" feelings, such as vulnerability, loss, guilt or fear. Because anger can give us energy, a sense of control, and the feeling of being able to fight back, those of us who are uncomfortable with vulnerability may use anger to mutate the threatening energy of those other feelings. Fixing this mutation is not difficult. It just requires the same approach as dealing with mutated confusion. We must simply look for and deal with the real feelings that are concealed by our anger.

On the other hand, a number of us will be afraid of anger itself. Since overwhelming experiences often involve painful lessons about the risks of expressing anger, many of us will feel compelled to transform the energy of anger into feelings that the psyche sees as less risky to express. Remember that the nuances of many abusive experiences often include the idea that allowing ourselves to be angry is tremendously dangerous. When these lessons go into storage along with the memory of the trauma, they become deeply imprinted on our psyche. A child being hurt by a violent parent knows instinctively that becoming angry would be very hazardous, so he represses this feeling. The anger goes into storage completely bound up with an intense sense of being in danger, a danger that would only increase if he were to express his feelings.

This combination of anger and the fear of expressing that anger not only encourages us to use mutation; it also makes undoing the habitual transformation somewhat more difficult. Since the connection between anger and danger is deeply imbedded in our subconscious belief system, our psyche learns to avoid expressing anger at all costs. As far as our subconscious is concerned, anger is not just psychologically unsafe, it is also physically dangerous. So our psyche finds especially creative ways to deal with it. Because the tendency to struggle with expressing anger is so common and because the psyche is so resourceful in avoiding this feeling, we will take some time to explore the ways our psyche defends against anger in more detail.

DEPRESSION: CLASSIC ANGER MUTATION

I've been told that I have a lot of repressed anger—whatever that means. I don't feel angry. I feel depressed. I cry a lot. Sure I have a temper sometimes, but who doesn't? People are so stupid, you know what I mean? I can't stand being around them. I hate being so alone. Why can't I find people who like me, who I can rely on? But I think the main problem is my depression.

—Cheryl B.

As we now know, depression has a number of different sources: biochemical imbalance, emotional drain from stored overwhelming experiences, and residual grief and sadness. Another cause of depression is mutated anger. Anger masquerading as depression is actually relatively common, because depression controls anger's energy so effectively. It simply collapses the psyche's energy in on itself, imploding to keep from exploding. On the surface, mutated anger looks exactly like any other form of depression, but fortunately, there are ways to tell the difference. One option is to look at whether or not we are comfortable with anger in general. As with all transformed emotions, our need to avoid triggering buried anger will cause us to avoid acknowledging it in day-to-day life.

Another option is to pay attention to when we started feeling down. If a particular event, such as a divorce or the death of a parent, seems to have prompted the depression, it is most likely due to either unresolved anger or sadness. In order to determine which of these is the cause, we just need to pay attention to the timing of our tears and lack of energy. What specific aspects of our situation cause us to feel down? For example, if we cry about a breakup, do we cry while remembering the good times or when we focus on our partner's history of cheating and lying? Do we feel depressed about our job because we have not achieved our career goals or because our boss treats us like a child? Knowing the specific context for feeling down will tell us if we are experiencing unresolved grief or mutated anger.

At times, of course, it will be hard to tell whether the real feeling behind our depression is grief or anger. Sometimes, we feel both. For example, we may feel down about the loss of some friends both because we miss them and because they betrayed us. While grief combined with anger can be somewhat more difficult to vent, we simply need to be sure to vent every facet of our emotions. We must remember that completing integration through emotions requires that we identify and integrate all the true feelings involved.

DISPLACED ANGER

> I hated my mom. It sounds weird, because my dad was the one who abandoned us. It wasn't really her fault, though I sure saw it that way. I would fantasize about him coming for us. Boy, was I in for a shock! One day we saw him in a store, and I ran up to him like he was a conquering hero. He acted like I didn't exist. He was embarrassed by me. And the really weird thing is, in my eyes, even that was my mom's fault. I refused to see what a jerk he was.
> —Tony B.

Mutation is not the psyche's only last-ditch option for avoiding the expression of threatening emotions, especially anger. It can also use misdirection—another incredibly effective and convoluted defense. Like mutation, misdirection sabotages expression in very subtle ways, but this defense involves identifying an incorrect reason for the correct feeling. With misdirection, we ignore the true source of our emotion and find other issues or people to blame. Though it can be used to help us cope with any threatening feeling, one of the most commonly misdirected emotions is anger. In a classic displaced anger scenario, someone who was harmed by an abusive father becomes incredibly angry with his or her mother. Although abuse survivors often have valid reasons to feel angry with mothers who failed to protect them, this legitimate version is different from displaced anger. In the latter, we feel explosive rage toward the non-abusive parent and no anger at all toward the abuser. In other words, we misdirect our anger toward the safer adult.

In spite of how irrational displaced anger might be, our psyche is amazingly adept at convincing us that it is justified. It is surprisingly easy to be completely taken in by the shifting of anger away from a violent person and onto someone or something else. Usually, we do not even notice that appropriate outrage is missing, and when we do, we find excuses for our apathy by saying that the abuser did not mean to hurt us or that we have forgiven him or her. These justifications, especially the idea of forgiveness, seem reasonable on the surface, but there is a difference between the intellectual decision to forgive—not seeking retribution—and emotional forgiveness, which requires that we resolve our anger.

While we may indeed choose to intellectually forgive a perpetrator, far too often we ignore the signs that we have not worked through our feelings. If we cannot comfortably discuss our anger, are consumed with rage over minor day-to-day problems, or are unable to forgive another person who was indirectly involved, chances are that we are simply using misdirection. In order to truly heal, we need to acknowledge our anger's real source. However, this is not an easy task. Just as we can have trouble seeing the real feelings hidden by mutation, seeing through our psyche's deception and dealing with the real cause of our feelings can be an uphill battle, especially when the psyche misdirects anger at ourselves.

SELF-DIRECTED ANGER

> *If my family knew that I hit myself, they would probably lock me up and throw away the key. I don't remember when it started. Even as a child I would punch myself—hard, none of these little love taps. But I've always been really good at hiding it. I guess I learned it from Dad—never hit where people can see. It's gotten worse since my husband asked for a divorce. I just feel like it's all my fault. Whenever I get mad or upset, I end up black and blue.*
>
> *—Jan B.*

Self-directed anger is a special form of misdirection that involves pointing anger at others back at ourselves. Anger at ourselves for a fault or a mistake seems as logical as anger at someone else, and we may be able to think of situations that seem to support this notion. However, the human psyche is simply not designed to be *genuinely* irate with itself, except in extreme circumstances. In the vast majority of cases, anger with ourselves is nothing more than misdirection. The evidence of this is the incredible difficulty we have resolving self-directed anger. Since we are not venting our anger at the correct source, we are unable to achieve closure. Think of those people dealing with self-directed anger again: chances are that they have been struggling with their anger for some time.

Self-directed anger takes many forms. Sometimes, it involves blaming ourselves for problems that were beyond our control; sometimes, it means not allowing ourselves to be happy. It can also fuel self-destructive obsessions, like cutting, eating disorders or suicidal thoughts. In any of its forms, however, this self-destructiveness is again—in spite of all appearances to the contrary—a protective mechanism. Our psyche is using self-directed anger to protect us from the expected consequences of directing our anger towards the true cause. When attempting to disable mutation and misdirection, it is critical to remember that in spite of the problems these defenses cause, our psyche believes that facing the real emotion or target would be much worse than continuing to rely on substitutions.

EXERCISE 7 - 2

Although problems with mutation and misdirection are not universal, they are fairly common. Think about the topics just discussed: do any apply to you? Do you use confusion to distract yourself from other feelings about painful events? Do you feel anger when another emotion would be more appropriate? Do you feel depressed when thinking about issues that might generate anger for others (or vice versa)? Do you feel excessive anger toward someone other than an abuser, or are you frequently angry at yourself? If any of these issues apply to you, write them down in your journal and discuss them with your counselor.

THE DILEMMA OF ANGER EXPRESSION

I can remember the exact moment like it was a minute ago. Never in my life had I been mad at my dad. Never. Then, one day in the middle of a session, there it was, just like it had always been there: rage. Full-blown, all-out, unadulterated rage. I had never felt anything like it. It was kind of scary. Getting it out was hard, 'cause it kept going away, but I will never forget the first time I actually felt it.

—Beth A.

As we have seen, anger is the most likely emotion to be mutated and misdirected, because it is often seen as the most dangerous. The sense of peril accompanying anger also gives it another distinction: unlike most emotions, anger can remain difficult to express, even after we have disabled our defenses. With other mutated and misdirected feelings, identifying the real emotion or source allows us to proceed with expression. Once we know what we are really feeling and why, we can use the standard steps to express it. However, anger that is left over from abusive experiences will often continue to be so frightening that typical venting will not work, especially when we are attempting to use physically expressive methods.

Even though we usually think of yelling or hitting as normal ways to express rage, these tactics are ineffective when dealing with anger that the psyche sees as dangerous. Going on a rampage will inevitably trigger the nuance of peril and the defense of mentally disconnecting. We may literally scare ourselves out of the feeling by venting it. Fortunately, we do not need to release our rage in one big scary leap. Expression can be broken down into tiny non-threatening steps. We can start with simply talking or even thinking about being angry and work our way up to making a list of issues that cause us to feel irritated, or listen as another person talks about feeling angry on our behalf. In the process, we gradually acclimate ourselves to the idea that venting anger is safe.

In deciding how to express anger, the key issue is to avoid triggering the impulse to disconnect. Remember that we must physically feel emotions in order to resolve them. If we disconnect and go numb, all the screaming and pounding in the world will accomplish nothing. We have to find a balance between sidestepping anger expression entirely and venting so intensely that we cannot stay connected. Our counselor is a critical asset in negotiating this middle ground. He or she can help us decide how to effectively express our feelings and can keep us grounded by providing reassurance and encouragement while we vent.

We will also need our counselor's assistance in recognizing and dealing with another challenge that may follow the venting of anger: a fear backlash. A fear backlash is due to the familiar troublesome connection between anger and danger. Because stored nuances from past traumas tell us to expect horrible consequences for expressing anger, we may feel intense anxiety after venting. This anxiety can in turn be mutated into other feelings, such as guilt or discomfort. We may even find ourselves feeling extremely bored, although we were tremendously upset just moments before. Contrary to appearances, however, the guilt, restlessness or boredom are simply due to the fear attached to our anger.

Dealing with a fear backlash, should it occur, is an important step in the process of expressing anger. After venting, we need to address any nuances or fears that may have been triggered and make sure that we are totally grounded and oriented before the end of our session. We must be certain that our psyche is not still anticipating terrible consequences for expressing anger. Like a time traveler, we need to bring ourselves totally back to the present, rather than leaving part of our psyche in the past. Facing this backlash can be uncomfortable, but on the other hand, the fear is a positive sign: it indicates that we have indeed identified the true feeling and the correct cause. We will encounter a fear backlash only if we are expressing real anger at a real target.

THE DOWNSIDE OF INTEGRATION

I really like the idea of cleaning out my closet. The stress of carrying around all that I've been through is getting to me, but I don't know if I can. Right now is not a good time to go digging through all that pain. It's a real Catch 22: either I feel more stressed now or I continue carrying around that junk and take the chance of feeling more stressed later. It's a tough decision.

—Chris M.

The possibility of having to face any of the problems outlined in this or the previous chapter may seem a little daunting, but it is important to remember they do not happen every time we express feelings or even every time we vent anger. Still, being aware of how our psyche can undermine expression helps us recognize and deal with potential obstacles quickly and effectively. Just as driving a car requires that we prepare for problems that happen only occasionally, knowing potential barriers to using emotions as a tool for integration will help us deal with any complications that may come up. When it works well, however, integrating through emotions allows us to completely resolve an overwhelming experience—either past or present—such that we totally eliminate the painful emotions and truly put that experience in the past.

The benefits and simplicity of using emotions to integrate events are especially obvious in dealing with recent overwhelming situations that are not triggering or otherwise connected with past events. During particularly painful current situations, integrating with emotions can easily help us finish the job that our psyche is unable to do on its own, and thus keep the experience from being placed in storage. Making a conscious effort to deal with those painful emotions—by identifying the source, feeling the emotion in our body, and expressing it directly—is often all that is needed to ensure that they do not become part of our psyche's backlog of unresolved problems.

However, integrating *past* experiences using emotions is not usually this simple. There is a reason our mind has avoided these feelings: they are uncomfortable and threatening. Facing them—integrating them—is often exhausting and distressing. While this approach is still the most direct and thorough way to eliminate problem reactions, it can sometimes require a sizable financial and emotional commitment, and there are times when digging up past painful feelings is not wise. In particular, we should be cautious about addressing past events if we are still in an abusive situation. In such cases, our first priority must be safety. We should worry about our past only if it is the reason we cannot remove ourselves from our current unsafe situation.

In addition to abusive situations, there are other times when integration may not fit our needs. Perhaps, like Chris, we do not have the energy or resources available. In these cases, we may simply want to improve our storage capacity or find healthier ways to avoid buried events. We may also want to use another, less painful and more indirect method of integrating experiences. Fortunately, we have many other tools in our psyche's toolbox. We can always use another aspect of who we are to help us integrate, store or avoid those buried experiences.

Chapter Eight

REORGANIZING, REINFORCING, REMOVING, AND OTHER CLOSET TRICKS

Great men are they who see that the spiritual is stronger than any material force—that thoughts rule the world.
—Ralph Waldo Emerson

Integrating experiences using emotions is certainly an effective way to eliminate our monsters, but it should never be mistaken for our only option. We have many choices in the psyche's toolbox and many ways to put these options to use. Any of the remaining aspects of who we are—our thoughts, behaviors, capacity for insight, subconscious abilities and innate physiological responses—can help with healing. If we are resourceful, we can creatively employ different tools to achieve any of the psyche's goals. We can also use the same tool for various purposes, or even combine tools to increase their effectiveness.

When we know how to use the different aspects of ourselves to achieve the psyche's goals, the only limits to their usefulness are our creativity and willingness to try something new. Each aspect of our "self" is adept at completing some portion of the psyche's functions. As we have seen, emotions are preferable for integration. Other tools can help with integration as well but are especially useful for increasing our ability to store and avoid events. There are even tools that sidestep the problems in our closet and change our emotional state without addressing our history at all. Notice, however, that we must know how these tools function. When we understand the various options, we can find the most appropriate path to recovery, make informed choices, and take an active role in controlling or eliminating the monsters in our closet.

INSIGHT

> *Looking at the reasons I do things has helped me feel a lot more in control and grounded. It's taken some time, but I feel like I know myself so much better than I did, like I'm comfortable in my skin. Sometimes, I still get irrational, but it doesn't happen nearly as much, and when it does, I can usually get my feet back under me relatively quickly. I can't tell you how nice it is to know who I am.*
> —*Ester F.*

As human beings, we have a natural desire to understand ourselves, our emotions and our thoughts. We want insight into why we do the things we do, not only to satisfy our intrinsic curiosity but also as a tool for emotional healing. Insight helps us see the underlying reasons for our reactions. Sometimes, this awareness into our motives centers on the basic overall dynamics of the psyche—this book, for example, attempts to provide this type of insight into various general concepts. More often, however, the tool of insight is more personal and focuses on understanding the specific events, issues and drives that form the bedrock of our own individual emotional problems.

This ability to see the mechanisms behind our behavior helps us heal in a variety of ways. On one level, it provides reassurance that our reactions are not random, which, in turn, decreases our overall anxiety level. Seeing that our emotions and actions are not bizarre and unpredictable helps us relax and accept ourselves. As a result, insight often helps us, like Ester, feel more grounded and comfortable. It gives us a quiet sense of being centered and calm, and best of all, the relaxation that comes from self-understanding is relatively permanent and does not require the upkeep that other forms of stress management often do.

Understanding the reasons for our reactions also makes them easier to control. When we recognize the trigger for negative feelings and thoughts, it takes less effort to keep them in storage. For example, someone who understands that the anger he feels whenever he is criticized is actually due to unpleasant experiences with his mother will have an easier time keeping that anger in perspective and not overreacting. Like organizing a cluttered closet, knowing where our emotions and thoughts fit amongst the compartments of our psyche makes them easier to contain. Furthermore, since we know the source of our reactions, when they do "fall out," we can quickly put them back.

In addition to decreasing our overall anxiety and helping us avoid, or at least contain, triggered reactions, insight can also help with integration. Obviously, the process of identifying the painful experiences behind our problem reactions is important when we want to vent our feelings. However, even when we do not plan on expressing emotions, insight alone can sometimes initiate the integration of painful memories. At times, the very process of recognizing and discussing the source of negative reactions brings a rush of emotion. This flood of emotion—or emotional catharsis—may in itself spontaneously finish the processing of that event.

However, when using the tool of insight, we need to be careful to avoid the common trap of endlessly searching for explanations. Remember that focusing on resolving confusion is one way to hide from threatening emotions. In order to keep a search for insight from becoming a perpetual struggle with confusion, we must be sure that we deal with our feelings. Simply running away from the pain into our intellect will not help us heal and could ultimately be very detrimental. We should also remember that insight alone may not be enough to entirely integrate residual emotions, thoughts and behaviors from traumatic experiences. The victim of a violent rape may be perfectly clear about why she has panic attacks during sex, but knowing this will not make them go away.

COGNITIVE ABILITIES

I won't say that I am an entirely new man...but almost! Practically none of the things that I used to panic myself about are upsetting today. And when I at times return to my old perfectionism, I quickly find my shoulds and musts, kick the hell out of them again, and go right back to leading a productive and enjoyable life.
—Mike*

Our cognitive abilities are another important tool that, like insight, involve our thoughts. However, unlike insight's focus on helping us understand our reactions, our cognitive abilities help us change those reactions by restructuring our thoughts. This tool is based on the principle that changing the way we think, whether on a deep core level or just in terms of our day-to-day "automatic" negative thoughts, changes our feelings and responses. The most simplistic version of this tool is the old—and oddly effective—advice to "look on the bright side." However, most cognitive abilities are much more complicated and can be used to perform a wide variety of tasks, including integrating experiences, storing memories and even avoiding triggering stored data.

For example, the cognitive technique of "rescripting" can integrate residual beliefs about powerlessness that occur following a traumatic experience. It accomplishes this task by changing the images and thoughts connected with the trauma. In other words, we consciously change how we see the experience to eliminate our sense of powerlessness. The process of changing our view of the event might involve picturing ourselves as bigger than the perpetrator—big enough to protect ourselves—or perhaps imagining that the abuser is in jail or otherwise incapacitated. By envisioning ourselves as more powerful than someone who hurt us, we address the perception of helplessness that we experienced during the event and consequently overcome the residual helplessness that we experience in everyday life (Burns, 2000).

---

* From Albert Ellis, *How to Make Yourself Happy and Remarkably Less Disturbable*, Impact Publishers (Atascadero, CA, 1999); used here with permission.

Most cognitive techniques, however, including Mike's method of kicking the hell out of his "shoulds" and "musts," focus on controlling our thoughts. Since negative current thoughts can trigger negative stored emotions, focusing on positive thoughts in the here and now helps us avoid the junk in our trauma closet. For example, if the thought that we should be perfect is connected with a buried sense of failure, avoiding the idea that we need to do things flawlessly helps keep that old shame in the closet. By learning to identify and replace negative thoughts in our current situation, we avoid triggering similar buried feelings.

Cognitive techniques can also help us step back out of the closet when day-to-day experiences happen to spontaneously bring up those irrational thoughts and feelings. Unless we are in the rare position of having completely integrated every life event, unprocessed data is bound to be triggered occasionally. Cognitive techniques' talent for bringing us back to "now" helps us cope with this occasional triggering. Since this tool forces us to re-connect with our intellect and examine whether or not our beliefs conform to current reality, cognitive techniques allow us to leave the closet, close the door and quickly regain control of our reactions.

Our cognitive abilities also provide a fabulous method of avoiding the closet and moving forward. Affirmations, for example, give us a road map to a healthier outlook and help our psyche rehearse positive rational thoughts, making them more likely to recur in the future. Although these positive statements may be contradicted by negative thoughts that sneak out of our closet, the conscious effort to disconnect from the negativity and remain grounded in the present pushes us in the right direction. Goal-setting is another cognitive technique that encourages progress. A goal provides a sense of direction that is immune to the chaos of our personal history. It helps us focus on the future and avoid the monsters from the past.

Although cognitive techniques address many different needs, they are particularly effective when we are emotionally or mentally stuck, such as during a deep depression. They also are very adept at breaking habitual patterns of negative thinking and come in handy when we must cope on a long-term basis with painful issues that, for whatever reason, we are unable to resolve. However, it is important to remember that cognitive techniques usually require upkeep. Occasionally, shifts in thinking patterns become permanent, but in most cases, our psyche is inevitably drawn back into the closet. As Mike found, changing our way of thinking requires ongoing effort.

EXERCISE 8 - 1

Look at your list of irrational thoughts from Chapter 4 and pick two or three that you would like to change. Next, identify the distortions in these thoughts (there are numerous lists of Cognitive Distortions—one such list is in Dr. David Burns' *The Feeling Good Handbook*), or you can try to identify the reason these thoughts are so disturbing. For example, if you believe that you will never be loved, you should ask how that would affect you and what it would mean if it were true. By following these assumptions to their logical conclusions, you can find and deal with the underlying beliefs that cause your irrational thoughts to be disturbing and scary.

SUBCONSCIOUS AND IMAGINATION

The thought of having a little girl inside me who held my feelings from the past seemed so outrageous that I figured there was no harm in humoring my therapist. But the minute I pictured her, I got the shock of my life. Tears started flowing. I FELT her. I know that sounds nuts. I even wondered if I had multiple personality disorder. But I guess I don't. My therapist said that we all have that little girl or boy inside us.

—Barbara R.

The tools of our subconscious and imagination allow us to visualize using any aspect of our self to complete any function, and as a result, they are probably the most flexible of all the tools in our psyche's toolbox. For example, we can use hypnosis—the purest application of the subconscious and imagination—to integrate feelings by picturing ourselves venting emotions. We can avoid the issues in our closet by establishing cues—such as holding our fingers in a particular way, or saying certain words—for pleasant images and feelings that allow us to relax and let go of our anxiety, or we can store experiences more effectively with containment exercises that involve imagining memories going into a secure bank vault. The possibilities with this tool are endless.

The key to hypnosis's flexibility is its talent for overcoming the mental barrier between reality and fantasy. Containment exercises work, because our psyche believes that the bank vault holding the memories exists. When we imagine placing a perpetrator in jail, our anxiety decreases, because the prison cell is "real." While this ability to confuse reality and fantasy is helpful in many contexts, it is a serious problem when we try to use hypnosis for memory retrieval—a popular, but risky, application. Because hypnosis blurs the line between reality and fantasy, it allows the psyche to create false memories to distract and protect us from our real history. In using hypnosis, therefore, we need to remember that its greatest gift, and also its greatest drawback, is its ability to alter reality.

In addition to hypnosis, guided imagery is another wonderful way to employ our subconscious and imagination as a healing tool. Guided imagery can also integrate, store and avoid events in our closet. This technique—which is less intense and less enveloping than hypnosis—involves simply relaxing and creating mental pictures that help us deal with experiences. Although the technique was not identified by name, we have already discussed using guided imagery during venting to imagine confronting another person. We have also mentioned the possibility of using guided imagery to see ourselves as more powerful than a perpetrator during a rescripting exercise.

Another creative and effective form of guided imagery, called inner-child work, helps us overcome our innate avoidance of childhood feelings, so we can access and integrate past events more easily. This technique involves connecting with and processing buried feelings by imagining a child version of ourselves who remembers painful events from our early years (Bradshaw, 1990; Whitfield, 1987). Because inner-child work focuses on accessing the feelings of our "little child," it avoids the common, but inaccurate, expectation that emotions from childhood events will be similar to the adult emotions that we experience every day. In the process, it short-circuits the strong tendency to run from feelings of being young and overwhelmed.

As we have seen, the subconscious and imagination can be used with a wide variety of therapeutic techniques and to address a great number of issues. The flexibility of these tools is a tremendous asset if ever we find that sidestepping the issues in our closet is our best option at the moment. In addition to using the subconscious and imagination to encourage relaxation—for example, by visualizing that we are relaxing on a beach—we can also use them to promote behavior changes, like quitting smoking or losing weight, or to imagine practicing the skills discussed in Chapter 10, so we can learn them more quickly. However, the subconscious and imagination are not the only tools we can use to change behavior while sidestepping the closet. There is also the particular forte of behavioral techniques.

BEHAVIORAL TECHNIQUES

> *I turned my son into a slob. When he was little, he would often leave things lying around, and I would clean up after him. At first, it was no big deal. I thought he was just little. But it got out of hand. I started feeling like a slave, and he did nothing for himself. Eventually, I realized that I was rewarding his slobbish behavior by cleaning up after him. When I stopped doing his job for him and started thanking him for doing it himself, suddenly I had a neat son. Yeah!!!!!*
>
> —Marcia G.

The tools discussed so far have primarily addressed or lightly sidestepped the issues in our closet. Behavioral techniques, on the other hand, use the basic principles of human learning to change our actions while avoiding underlying issues altogether. On the surface, these principles, which go by such strange names as aversive conditioning, reinforcement, and extinction, may seem exotic, but in reality, they are very commonplace. For example, a recovering alcoholic who takes medication to feel nauseated when he drinks is relying on aversive conditioning. When we ignore a nagging spouse hoping he or she will stop, we are counting on extinction, and parents who give their child a treat for good behavior are using reinforcement.

For the most part, behavioral techniques focus exclusively on tangible activities. We encourage desired conduct and punish or ignore behaviors that we want to eliminate. However, a few behavioral techniques do address feelings by doing away with the associated physical discomfort while still avoiding our closet. For example, one treatment for phobias, called systematic desensitization, involves learning to relax when we are exposed to reminders of our fear. First, we are taught ways to reduce our anxiety in the presence of a distant likeness, such as a tiny mental image of the phobia trigger. Then, step by step, we move closer to the real source of our fear, until our phobia has been mastered.

Although systematic desensitization and other behavioral techniques can sometimes be helpful with eliminating some problems while keeping the closet door shut, this tool's primary focus is changing conduct. As most parents know, behavioral techniques are unbeatable in this context. When thoughts and emotions are not contributing to the problem, behavioral techniques provide practical and efficient ways to manage certain negative reactions and to reinforce the progress made using other tools. The benefit—and also the shortcoming—of behavioral approaches is that they do not address the effect of our deeper selves on behavior. However, there are tools that do address these more intricate issues.

EXERCISE 8 - 2

Since the subconscious, imagination and behavioral techniques can be helpful in most situations, consider talking to your counselor about finding ways to use them to help your healing process. They can be used to increase your ability to relax, improve access to childhood traumas, and discourage some problem reactions while you are addressing the underlying issues. You can also use systematic desensitization to overcome certain phobias, even of facing particularly difficult experiences. You may also want to develop ways to reward yourself after completing particularly difficult treatment tasks or after addressing especially challenging issues.

OTHER TECHNIQUES FOR INTEGRATION

It's funny how much certain things remind us of the past. When my therapist asked me to bring my old stuffed dog to therapy, I thought she was nuts, but boy did that dog take me back to when I was little! Once I got over being embarrassed about cuddling Puddles in public, it was like I went back in time. I think that one thing saved me about two years' worth of therapy.

—Dave L.

In addition to the behavioral techniques that do not touch issues in our closet, there are a number of activities that encourage our psyche to deal with past events. Play therapy, for example, is an activity that accesses an inborn method of integrating experiences. Children naturally play to process information and deal with feelings, so engaging in play allows us to work through painful situations in an instinctive way (Levy, 1976; Oaklander, 1978). Although play therapy is most often used with children, adults can also use toys, stuffed animals and crayons to process feelings and memories, especially those that occurred in childhood.

Writing and journaling are excellent behavioral options for integrating events. Keeping a journal of both past and current experiences is a remarkably effective way to allow our psyche to digest painful issues. The very act of writing down the details of an experience—lingering over our thoughts and feelings—taps into the psyche's natural processing abilities. Journaling lets us safely vent feelings and puts difficult times into perspective, and the very process of thinking about an experience while finding the words to express our thoughts and feelings gives our psyche time to work towards integration (Freinkel, Fuerst and Krieger, 1999).

Another creative option to aid processing is non-dominant handwriting. This technique, which involves writing with the hand we do not normally use, is discussed in the book *The Power of Your Other Hand*, by Lucia Capacehione. Writing in this unusual way seems to access and integrate childhood experiences and is surprisingly effective, especially when combined with such reminders of childhood as crayons. No one is exactly sure why using our non-dominant hand brings up past feelings with such ease. It is possible that the awkwardness of this activity reminds us of

124

what it felt like to write as a child, or it may be that non-dominant hand work taps into our brain's innate processing abilities.

Non-dominant hand work, of course, is not the only form of therapy that accesses the brain's natural processing abilities. In fact, it could be argued that every therapy does this on some level. The act of helping the psyche complete the functions that it cannot accomplish on its own is really nothing more than a way of consciously accessing our psyche's ability to heal itself. In the next chapter, we will discuss a number of somewhat more complex techniques that are more specifically focused in this direction. These therapies use one final tool for healing: the natural capacity of both our brain and body to integrate, store and avoid overwhelming experiences.

Chapter Nine

METATHERAPIES

..o. **NiGHTMARES** ARE JUST THE MiND'S WAY OF TAKiNG OUT THE EMOTiONAL GARBAGE FROM THE DAY BEFORE!

www.ucomics.com TOM WiLSON & TOM II ¹²/₄

I n the past few decades, a new category of therapy has evolved with an entirely distinct approach to healing. These extraordinary "metatherapies" transcend conventional approaches to recovery by accessing our inborn mental and physical capacity to heal. Using a number

---

of the tools already discussed and some treatments that we would probably not normally associate with mental health therapy—such as tapping acupressure points—the metatherapies take advantage of the fact that our psyche is indeed built to heal itself. These therapies, with their creative use of the brain's and the body's natural abilities, may well represent the beginning of a revolution in mental health.

Since the methods used by these therapies are somewhat atypical, there may be questions about their effectiveness—a legitimate concern if they have not yet been thoroughly researched. However, most of these therapies have been around for decades and have shown great clinical results. Some, like EMDR, have also been extensively tested and have proven to be very effective, while others have yet to gain sufficient acceptance in the field to be objectively researched. Once given a fair trial, however, it is likely that these therapies will come to be viewed as valuable tools for healing. Whether or not we plan to use these techniques in our recovery, we owe it to ourselves to see what they have to offer.

EYE MOVEMENT DESENSITIZATION AND REPROCESSING (EMDR)

> *Even though I had been told about the technique, I didn't expect it to be so intense. He started waving his fingers in front of my eyes and suddenly, I was there again. I was a child: cold, alone, tired, and then it was gone, and I was watching my dad hit my brother. Every time we triggered something new, it was like being there all over again. And then it would fade. Afterwards, I was exhausted but at peace. I never would have expected to cover that much so quickly.*
>
> *—Margaret H.*

Undoubtedly the most prominent and thoroughly researched of the metatherapies is Eye Movement Desensitization and Reprocessing (EMDR). This technique was discovered by a psychologist named Francine Shapiro, who noticed that if our eyes move rapidly back and forth while we think about a disturbing issue, our discomfort with that issue decreases. Over the past few decades, Shapiro and others have worked diligently to ensure that EMDR was thoroughly researched. They have also made many modifications to improve its outcome, the most notable of which is the inclusion of cognitive-behavioral therapy techniques. Today, it is the most extensively researched treatment for Post-Traumatic Stress Disorder in the history of counseling and is considered a powerful way to address a wide variety of emotional problems (Rothbaum, 1997; Wilson, Becker and Tinker, 1995, 1997).

Two principal concepts of EMDR are that the psyche is capable of identifying and processing unresolved issues and that we can trigger this integration through a process called bilateral stimulation—the current modification of the original eye movement procedure. At its most simplistic, bilateral stimulation involves drawing our attention back and forth from the right side of the body to the left, normally using the eyes, the ears or the sense of touch. In other words, clients either watch a visual cue move from right to left, or they hear a noise or feel a touch on alternating sides of their bodies. In a typical EMDR session, therefore, we focus on a disturbing symptom or memory, do bilateral stimulation, and allow issues to surface, one after another, until the identified problem is resolved (Chemtob, et al., 2000).

Although scientists have documented the effectiveness of EMDR in many studies and have put considerable effort into trying to determine the causal mechanism, there is still a great deal of uncertainty and numerous theories about how EMDR "reprocesses" our experiences. One theory to explain EMDR is that it creates a forced state of relaxation, encouraging us to connect relaxation, rather than anxiety, to the traumatic memories. Another hypothesis that has been considered is that dividing our attention between the bilateral stimulation and the memory of the trauma forces us to "drop" our negative feelings about the event.

However, one of the most reasonable explanations for EMDR's effectiveness is that the bilateral stimulation, which forces mental activity to move between the two hemispheres of the brain, triggers a biological mechanism for moving memories out of short-term, episodic storage in the brain's limbic system. There are many scientific studies on this esoteric subject, but the connection between bilateral shifting and integration is also readily apparent in everyday life. When we try to understand the details of a complicated concept, for instance, our eyes often automatically move back and forth. Rapid Eye Movement (REM) sleep—the stage of sleep when our eyes move rapidly from side to side—is another example of this connection, since this is when we seem to integrate day-to-day experiences.

This link between REM sleep and integration also suggests a possible reason that overwhelming events are not integrated in the first place and an explantion of how EMDR helps correct the problem. As we know, traumatic or painful experiences disturb our sleep and give us nightmares—most likely a side effect of the psyche's attempts at integration. The resulting disruption, in turn, undoubtedly further interferes with the integration process: we certainly cannot expect to continue dreaming if we are awakened due to a nightmare. On the other hand, there is no danger of an EMDR session being interrupted in this way, regardless of how distressing the issue may be. As a result, EMDR gives us a chance to complete the integration that we could not finish while sleeping.

Although we may want to try EMDR on our own, in reality, this apparently simple procedure involves risks. Some people using EMDR experience overpowering feelings similar to those that occur during a flashback or a nightmare. So EMDR should be attempted only with the guidance of a trained counselor. Even with this help, we may find that at times our subconscious fights accessing these feelings and issues, causing us to suddenly "go blank" during a session. On rare occasions, the intense emotions can even exacerbate certain health problems, such as asthma or high blood pressure, and the distressing feelings may not stop when the session is over. They can surface between sessions as well, increasing urges to be self-destructive or to relapse with an addiction.

For these reasons, when using EMDR we must be particularly meticulous about communicating clearly with our counselor regarding our reactions to the treatment process, and have a plan for crisis situations that may come up between sessions. We must also be certain that our counselor is qualified to provide this treatment. Even counselors who are familiar with other therapies should not use EMDR unless they have had formal training in this particular area. A therapist who is properly trained in EMDR is equipped to help us deal with the intense reactions that this technique can generate. While most people undergoing EMDR treatment do not experience strong emotions, taking the proper precautions will allow us to enjoy the many well-documented benefits of EMDR without putting ourselves at risk.

THE MERIDIAN ENERGY THERAPIES

After I broke up with Jean, I had trouble sleeping. I was SO angry. Even though I was glad it was over, I would wake up at 1:00 or 2:00 in the morning and all I could think about was how she treated me. I wanted to kill her. But then my therapist taught me the tapping. Whenever I'd wake up, I'd just do it for a few minutes. It helped me let go, and I'd relax. Before long, I wasn't even waking up any more.

—Mimi J.

The energy therapies are not so much a new treatment as an innovative application of an ancient Eastern approach to healing. Therapies that manipulate the body's bioelectrical field—either the entire field, such as with Reiki; or through the meridians, as with acupuncture—have been around for centuries, but using them to address emotional issues is relatively new, at least in our culture. Meridian energy therapies involve balancing or manipulating the messages passed along the bioelectrical field's meridians—a communication pathway between the brain and the body not terribly unlike the spinal column. In the medical field, for example, this form of treatment might be used to interrupt a message about pain during surgery. In a psychotherapeutic setting, practitioners attempt to clear away disturbances—or stuck information—in the bioelectrical field by tapping or touching certain spots on the body, such as below the collarbone.

Although the notion that our body can exert such a powerful influence on our emotions may initially seem strange to our Western way of thinking, the idea that energy meridians can be used to treat emotional problems makes a great deal of sense. On a basic level, emotions are little more than physical responses to electrical impulses passed along particular nerve pathways. We may even have felt these messages on occasion, such as during a scary movie: the music warns us of impending doom, our anxiety level rises, and—aaahhh!! a bloody zombie attacks out of nowhere, sending a bolt of electric fear running through our body. Since that shock, and any other messages about emotions, obviously must follow predictable pathways, the idea that we could alter our feelings by interrupting those messages is not so bizarre.

The goal of all meridian energy therapies is to do just that—to regulate the body's messages about emotional issues by touching or tapping acupressure points—but each energy therapy goes about achieving this goal in different ways. Thought Field Therapy (TFT), for example, uses a specific combination of points for each emotion. To address rage, we would first tap the eyebrows and then an inch under the collarbone. Addressing abandonment would involve a different set of tapping spots, and so on. Another important concept in TFT is that food toxins or chemical allergies interfere with the release of emotional problems. If emotions do not dissipate quickly, a TFT counselor will often attempt to identify what might be blocking the energy field (Callahan, 1996).

The method used by TFT is an excellent example of the overall meridian energy therapy approach, but each of these therapies has its own individual style. For example, Emotional Freedom Technique (EFT) differs from TFT in that it uses just one pattern of points for any issue being addressed—a pattern which contains all the points used by TFT plus several others. We identify the issue to be addressed by making a verbal statement prior to tapping (Craig and Fowlie, 1995). Another meridian energy therapy that uses an even more distinct approach is Tapas Acupressure Technique (TAT), which requires that we press several acupressure points at once. These are only a few of the more common meridian energy therapies. There are others, and each has a different approach to identifying and addressing our various emotional issues.

In addition to using different methods of affecting the bioelectrical field, practitioners of the meridian energy therapies also have distinct views on the importance of life experiences. Some hold that we need to address overwhelming experiences only in a very limited way. In particular, Roger Callahan, who developed TFT, believes that it is unnecessary to deal extensively with past events, other than traumas. In his view, emotional problems have a physical basis that can be addressed directly by correcting the underlying disturbance in our energy field. Other meridian energy therapies, however, like EFT, focus more on identifying events that may be contributing to our emotional problems.

While we may be tempted to casually dismiss the seemingly ludicrous idea that we can simply tap away disturbing emotions, research indicates that the meridian energy therapies can have a significant impact not only on our emotions (Wylie, 1996), but on our body as well. For example, a recent study found that TFT can improve our heart rate variability, an aspect of our body's nervous system that is extremely difficult to affect (Callahan, 2001). Although few studies on TFT and EFT have been printed in journals published by established schools of therapy, clinical studies are available on websites, including www.tftrx.com and www.emofree.com.

As with every form of treatment, however, the meridian energy therapies do have their drawbacks—the biggest of which, oddly enough, is that many people tend to dismiss their effectiveness. Because these therapies are so simple and painless—and so novel—it is easy to find other explanations for any improvements that occur. Another concern with these therapies is that they do not always satisfy our need to talk about and mentally process issues and events. We would do well to remember that the meridian energy therapies focus on eliminating the emotional charge from an event rather than on processing; but after resolving other related issues, we may come to the conclusion that these therapies have truly helped us to let go of the past.

ASSISTED PROCESSING (AP)

When my therapist suggested that we do all that tapping while we talked, it seemed so crazy. But after just a few minutes, I knew something different was happening. I still don't totally get it...something about brain processing, energy meridians, whatever...but boy, did it work! I've been in counseling since I was 13, and I've never seen the kind of changes that I have in the last 9 months. I feel almost whole. I see myself acting and feeling like a person who believes in herself. And I know that I used to be

incapable of that. I've really grown and healed more than I ever
thought possible.

—*Elaina M.*

EMDR and the meridian energy therapies offer treatment approaches that are, in many ways, polar opposites. While EMDR accesses the brain's processing abilities using a method that can be very emotionally intense, the meridian energy therapies eliminate the emotional charge connected with events while sidestepping intellectual processing. A technique called Assisted Processing (AP) takes the middle ground between these approaches by combining aspects of these two techniques and adding standard talk therapy as well. During an AP session, clients talk about their concerns, tap acupressure points and do bilateral stimulation— simultaneously, separately, or in various combinations.

Although three different types of activities occurring at the same time might seem simply distracting rather than beneficial, the different components of AP combine and complement each other in synergistic ways. Talking about our issues helps us focus and gain insight, and bilateral stimulation encourages the rapid processing of events; at the same time, tapping the acupressure points decreases the intensity of our emotional distress, dissipating the emotional charge quickly. As a result, we can integrate very disturbing events much more painlessly than with either standard therapy or EMDR, while still achieving a sense of resolution and closure.

Although AP retains some of the benefits of its components, it is also different in a number of ways. For instance, unlike many meridian energy therapies, AP deals with past events very directly and is concerned with the effects of only a few energy toxins; and among other differences from EMDR, AP uses relatively slow, rather than rapid, movements from side to side. Slowing down the shifts is more than a simple change in procedure, because this also decreases the speed and intensity of the connections between thoughts. As a result, with AP, we cannot rely exclusively on subconscious associations to bring the events at the root of our problems to light. However, the slower shifts also reduce the risk that issues will surface between sessions—a terrific plus for some of us.

AP thus requires slightly different expectations than we might have if we were using its components separately. First and foremost, since our subconscious cannot be expected to identify relevant issues on its own, we will need to work more diligently with our therapist during AP to find the unprocessed experiences underlying our issues. We should also be prepared to deal with the emotional pain these issues bring up. AP often requires that we access, focus on, and integrate very disturbing memories and emotions. Most clients find that AP is not excessively uncomfortable, due to the combination of bilateral stimulation and tapping acupressure points, and when the processing does become painful, there are options for decreasing this discomfort.

NEUROLINGUISTIC PROGRAMMING/ COMPUTATIONAL LINGUISTICS (NLP/CL)

At first, I was really resistant to thinking about the accident again, but after I relaxed and imagined being in my favorite movie theater, I started to loosen up. Thinking about the beginning and end, when I was safe, helped too. But the weird part was going through it. It was like watching a video on fast forward: after the first couple times, it almost seemed funny. At the end of the session, I was tired, but calm. It was great.

—Fred J.

Neurolinguistic Programming (NLP) is perhaps one of the most well known of the metatherapies, having made its debut in the early 1970s. Although we may recognize NLP's name, we may not realize that one of its many techniques—Visual Kinesthetic Dissociation (VKD), otherwise known as the NLP phobia cure–is intended to "recode," or alter, the structure of traumatic memories, primarily through the use of guided imagery. With VKD, we must first relax and distance ourselves emotionally from the trauma. Usually, we accomplish this by picturing the event on a movie screen or seeing it in black and white. Another option might be to make any perpetrator that is involved seem absurd, for example, by dressing him in our mind as a clown. Next, we run through the memory, rapidly and in reverse, which decreases our negative feelings. Finally, we go back into the memory to find resources, learn lessons, and practice more productive responses.

As with most metatherapies, VKD has not been thoroughly researched, and there is a great deal of uncertainty about how it works. It is possible that VKD could simply be, as its name implies, a form of dissociation, a way of improving our ability to store and avoid the memory, which as we know has its downside. Leaving an unprocessed memory in storage, regardless of how well it is buried, can cause problems with psychic drain, numbing and blind spots. On the other hand, VKD is a relatively painless technique that has been used by various counselors for many years with relative success. In fact, other than the requirement that we must specify a particular trauma, one that we can remember well, it has few drawbacks.

TRAUMATIC INCIDENT REDUCTION (TIR)

One of the things I noticed about TIR was that when I first started going through the rape, I had more feelings about it, but after a while, I started thinking about it more rationally and understanding things better. Probably the nicest thing was how much I felt listened to and supported. I didn't feel rushed or judged at all. It was wonderful. And I was so amazed that it made such a difference to just think about it and talk about it. Afterwards, I felt totally different about the whole thing.

—Mary S.

While Traumatic Incident Reduction (TIR) is being introduced with the metatherapies, it looks so much like standard talk therapy that, for some of us, it may not even seem to qualify as a novel approach. However, in addition to basic talk, TIR incorporates a number of features that access the mind's innate ability to rapidly integrate overwhelming experiences. A TIR session consists of repeatedly thinking about—or "reviewing"—an event and then discussing the details during a highly structured interview with a TIR facilitator (either a professional counselor or lay practitioner). In other words, we go through the cycle of visualizing the event and talking about it with the facilitator over and over until it feels resolved (Coughlin, 1995).

TIR is based on the principle that integration is the natural outcome of examining an event in detail. Its practitioners believe that the only obstacle to spontaneous integration is our tendency to avoid thinking about painful experiences—a tendency which TIR's rounds of repeatedly reviewing and discussing an event attempt to overcome. However, in addition to this basic cycle, TIR also includes innovative procedures that help integration as well. For example, the rhythmic structure of the interview seems to create a relaxed state that facilitates processing, and TIR encourages us to look for earlier experiences that might be contributing to our intense reaction to the trauma. Finally, since a TIR session is not over until the trauma is resolved, the security of knowing that we will not be "left hanging" may also help with processing for some of us. Even if a session takes two or three hours, we can count on a sense of closure by the end (Stafford, 1999).

While these features help with integration, TIR still maintains a sense of familiarity and normality that may feel more palatable to those of us who are unsure about exotic techniques. An added appeal is that TIR addresses our painful experiences gradually. Because we take an active and conscious role in looking at the details of an experience, we can filter out excessively painful aspects of an event until we are ready to face them. However, if we choose to use TIR, we need to keep in mind that lay TIR facilitators are not trained to deal with complex emotional issues and should be consulted with caution. Also, if we want insurance to pay for our treatment, we must be sure that the extended two- to three-hour session will be covered.

We should be aware as well that TIR can potentially be extremely painful. Both components of this technique—thinking about the incident and talking to the facilitator—can be very upsetting. However, if we are concerned about a particular incident, have the time necessary to complete the process and are willing to deal with the intense emotions that can be generated, TIR is an extremely effective form of treatment. In addition to being relatively safe, this technique allows us to face painful issues gradually, using an approach that is more familiar than other metatherapies.

EXERCISE 9 - 1

The metatherapies are clearly not for everyone, but you may find that you could benefit from what they have to offer. Even if your counselor is not trained in the technique that you find appealing, there may be a trained practitioner in your area who is willing to work collaboratively to help you address a particular issue or event while you maintain your ongoing relationship with your current counselor.

A FULL TOOLBOX

This process has been more painful and almost as joyful as giving birth to twins...and has lasted a hell of a lot longer. Looking back, I see that I had an intense desire to destroy myself and all those I cared about. But doing the processing has made such a difference. Before I started working on my past, I was getting nowhere. Now I'm making a lot of progress. I feel like a different person.

—Tasha N.

EMDR, the meridian energy therapies, AP, VKD and TIR are excellent examples of the range and types of possible metatherapies, but they are only a few of the alternatives available in this area. There are scores of potential ways to use the mind and body's innate healing capacity still waiting to be discovered. This chapter has explored only the tip of the iceberg in terms of treatment options, and the scientific community has barely begun to look at issues of treatment effectiveness and underlying dynamics. At this point, we will need to vary our usual approach and settle for simply looking at the idiosyncrasies of the different possible metatherapies, rather than trying to grasp the bigger picture.

Although our inability to completely understand the underlying dynamics of the metatherapies might be seen as a disadvantage, we should be careful about dismissing them due to their peculiarities. Many innovations that we now consider incredibly beneficial, from x-ray machines to automobiles, were regarded as strange when they were introduced. Once the metatherapies have been properly tested and we overcome our initial discomfort, we may also view them as profoundly beneficial innovations as well. Even now, EMDR, in particular, has demonstrated its ability to resolve a wide variety of issues, and the others are showing encouraging clinical results. We would be doing ourselves a disservice if we did not take these therapies seriously when considering possible tools for recovery.

Now that we are familiar with how innate physiological responses can be used to heal emotional problems, our toolbox is complete. These tools—our emotions, thoughts, behaviors, capacity for insight, subconscious abilities and innate physiological responses—allow us to carry out the jobs of integration, storage and avoidance that our psyche was unable to finish on its own. However, clearly, recovery from emotional problems does not happen in a bubble. We all rely on certain skills and resources to help us through the healing process and to live a healthy life thereafter. Because these skills and resources are often damaged by the long-term effects of unprocessed events, even after we have tackled the beasts in our closets, we frequently find that there is still work to do.

Chapter Ten

INTERNAL AND EXTERNAL RESOURCES: STEPPING OUTSIDE THE CLOSET

Such happiness as life is capable of comes from the full participation of all our powers in the endeavor to wrest from each changing situation of experience its full and unique meaning.

—John Dewey

The various tools in our toolbox give us wonderful options for helping the psyche complete the integration, storage and avoidance of those experiences it cannot process on its own. However, when overwhelming events have been left in storage for many years or even decades, they often cause serious problems in our basic ability to deal with ourselves and the world around us. Just as a broken pipe causes water damage that does not just disappear after the leak is fixed, repairing our emotional health often requires more than simply stopping past events from continuing to affect our reactions. We also need to fix the damage that has been done to our overall functioning by repairing our support system, our life skills and our sense of self.

141

These skills and resources are not just the garnish for our recovery. They also have a tremendous positive or negative influence on our healing—because pluses in these areas help us make necessary changes while problems keep us stuck in destructive life patterns and increase the chance that we will be harmed again. In other words, traumatic events cause damage to our support system, life skills and sense of self, but traumas can also be caused *by* problems in these areas. For example, low self-esteem is a common reason for staying with an abusive spouse, but then, the abuse lowers the victim's self-esteem, increasing the chances that he or she will continue to tolerate the abuse. To take the leaky pipe analogy a step further, it is as if the dripping pipe damages the floorboards, and somehow the damaged floorboards then, in turn, cause another leak.

Healing thus often involves more than simply helping our psyche cope with buried experiences. We must also repair the damage done to our support system, life skills and sense of self. For some of us, fixing problems in these areas may require only a few minor adjustments. However, those of us who have been struggling for quite a while with numerous unprocessed experiences will most likely need to put considerable energy into addressing who is in our life, how we interact with the world and how we see ourselves. These are issues we cannot ignore. Mending the damage to our skills and resources is a critical aspect of our recovery.

SUPPORT SYSTEMS

I think that the hardest and most important part of my recovery was getting new friends. I must have relapsed 20 times before I decided that my sponsor was right: I had to stop clinging to my drinking buddies. I wanted to believe that I could still hang out with them and stay sober. Letting go was so painful. To be honest, it was the most difficult part of my recovery, but what a difference it has made!

—Michael I.

When considering resources that significantly influence our recovery, the most obvious is our support system—and clearly, one of the most critical aspects of that support system is the relationship that we have with our counselor. A positive, productive therapeutic relationship is a critical resource for our healing, especially when navigating the most treacherous parts of recovery. However, in order to make this relationship work, we must be willing to be vulnerable about our issues, feelings and reactions to the therapeutic process. As difficult as this type of openness can be, it is the foundation of a safe and speedy recovery.

Relationships with family and friends also seriously affect our healing, either positively or negatively. Those around us inevitably give us feedback about our healing, and this feedback can have a tremendous—if at times subconscious—effect. Our closest relationships can reinforce our progress, giving us the confidence we need to change. However, family and friends can also encourage us to stay stuck, especially when we are changing patterns that they are unable or unwilling to give up. This inability to accept our growth—no matter how subtly their disapproval may be communicated—can generate a surprising amount of uncertainty and self-doubt. We must be careful that these subtle digs do not make us want to give up on healing.

In addition to encouraging or discouraging progress, support systems also have an enormous impact on our sense of safety—a critical concern during recovery. We cannot heal when we do not feel safe. Stable relationships provide the security we need to take risks, a helpful benefit in itself, but this safety also encourages our psyche to relax, allowing painful issues from the past to surface more easily. As a result, healthy, positive relationships help us access and address our core issues more quickly and easily. Chaotic relationships, on the other hand, make us feel insecure and guarded, causing the psyche to shut down processing, which of course undermines recovery and sabotages progress.

However, our support system does not hold all the power in relation to recovery. Recovery often has a tremendous effect on our support system as well. As we become healthier, our needs and expectations in relationships can change dramatically. Positive changes to our stress level, addictive urges and emotional reactions can make relationships with long-time friends who are still trapped in those destructive patterns feel uncomfortable. In many cases, after some time in recovery, we will want to examine those we rely on most and possibly find new sources of support, especially if, like Michael, we are trying to overcome an addiction.

Unfortunately, finding people to embrace this developing self is not always easy. While we are learning new ways to cope, our social skills may be limited, and not every situation is ideal for hammering out interpersonal rough edges. One excellent solution to this problem is a support group. Like an incubator, a structured support group nurtures and encourages us until we are ready to face more challenging circumstances. The group's ground rules set limits on how members interact, giving us a chance to learn to connect with other people who support our positive changes, reinforce growth, and discourage negative patterns.

EXERCISE 10 - 1

Take a few minutes to evaluate your support system. First, list all those whom you consider your closest and dearest friends and relatives. Then, add those whom you do not necessarily lean on emotionally but who still have a great deal of influence over you, either due to financial reasons or because you are required to spend considerable time with them. Next to each of these names, list how you believe they would react if/when you achieve your emotional and therapeutic goals—once you become the person you would most like to be. It is important that you be completely honest about how changes in you will affect your relationship with each of them. Discuss this list with your counselor.

SPIRITUALITY

Bobbie wasn't supposed to die. I did everything right: got married in the church, went to mass on Sunday, even stayed married to Stan when I wanted to leave. I don't understand how God could have abandoned me and let my son die. God was supposed to watch over my family and me. I don't understand how this could

144

have happened. I prayed and prayed while Bobbie was in the hospital. How could this have happened?

—Ginnie B.

Spirituality is another source of support that often has an enormous influence on our healing. Whether we view spirituality as an internal resource or a relationship with an external deity, it provides comfort, guidance, and perspective during life's most difficult moments. Even in the midst of extreme turmoil, spirituality can give us a sense of peace and a healthy, productive outlook. It also sets ground rules about the rewards of living a good life and tells us what is expected from us, from life and from the transcendent. We may not consciously think about these rules and expectations, but they are the foundation for our sense of safety and purpose in the world (Gendlin, 1979).

While spirituality is normally a source of comfort and guidance, there are times when it can generate pain as well. Sometimes, an experience is traumatic primarily because it violates our spiritual rules— Ginnie, for example, subconsciously expected to be "taken care of" if she went to church and stayed married. Since our sense of safety in the universe is based on these kinds of expectations, we often feel incredibly threatened when the "rules" are violated, and if those violations are traumatic in themselves—as her son's death undoubtedly was for Ginnie—the unprocessed combination of painful emotions and spiritual confusion will stay with us indefinitely. It is no surprise, then, that a "crisis of faith" can leave us floundering and rudderless for years or even decades.

Our spirituality may also need healing if we believe that we have broken our own spiritual rules. In these situations, we can feel guilty, ashamed, and disconnected on a spiritual level. Our difficulties are compounded when the spiritual problem cannot be corrected; for instance, when someone who is Catholic gets a divorce, or when a gay man belongs to a religion that believes his sexual orientation is sinful. With no way to reconcile the conflict between our spiritual rules and the reality of who we are or what has happened, we may try to ignore either our spirituality or the "sin" that clashes with our beliefs. However, ignoring either will not resolve the situation. The ongoing battle between our beliefs and our experiences will continue to affect us, at least on a subconscious level.

145

Because spirituality is such a critical component of our identity, it may be difficult to acknowledge this struggle, even to ourselves—but ignoring internal conflict is rarely effective. Resolving a spiritual dilemma with quick answers (or, worse, with avoidance) keeps us from healing the cracks in our sense of safety and purpose. In spite of how deeply personal this issue might feel, it is critical that we address it with a counselor and/or a spiritual guide. Whether by resolving our feelings of shame, accepting the unpredictability of life, or finding a spirituality that speaks to our experiences, we must find a way to renew this important resource.

LIFE SKILLS

I hated being physically abused when I was a kid. I promised myself that I'd never act like my mom, but sometimes I'd get so mad with the kids that I thought I was going to lose it. So I went into therapy. I figured that once I had dealt with what happened, everything would be okay. But even after I worked through all the abuse, I still wasn't sure how to handle the kids. I knew what not to do, but I had no idea what to do.

—Jean C.

Unprocessed buried experiences also impact our functioning because they often influence the skills that we use to cope with day-to-day issues and problems. Many of us find that suppressing our monsters takes so much time and energy that we have little left for learning healthy ways to handle feelings, manage stress and interact appropriately with others. Also, the painful consequences of these events—triggered emotional reactions, numbing, depression, addictions and the like—usually do not respond to standard coping mechanisms, making these skills seem useless and unnecessary. As a result, over the course of a lifetime we often overlook important lessons in these areas.

For instance, the emotional chaos that results from non-integrated events can wreak havoc on our ability to deal with our feelings. The many years that we spend trying to control an unruly combination of past and current emotions often convince us that emotions are, by definition, unmanageable. Triggered overwhelming feelings obviously do not respond to such simple suggestions as "go for a walk" or "count to 10," so, over time, we learn to ignore this kind of common-sense advice. In the process, we fail to notice that such tactics do indeed work with normal, everyday feelings. Consequently, even after our old emotions have been resolved, we still may not know how to handle certain feelings—especially those we consider particularly unpleasant.

Notice, however, that difficulty with handling emotions does not usually apply to all feelings equally. We may feel perfectly comfortable managing fear or sadness, for example, while continuing to have serious difficulty with anger. These areas of comfort and competence give us the illusion that we have regained our ability to handle emotions. In reality, certain feelings can still be so distressing that we avoid acknowledging them altogether, making it likely that we will bury another batch of unresolved feelings. Learning to live a healthy life, therefore, requires that we evaluate our ability to manage the entire spectrum of feelings and develop a plan for coping with and expressing those that we are tempted to avoid.

Stress management is another critical life skill that is often seriously affected by buried unprocessed experiences. As we know, a backlog of buried feelings can make dealing with stress utterly impossible, due not only to residual unprocessed anxiety but also because our psyche must stay habitually wound up to keep stored memories on hold. Since buried experiences are more likely to surface when we are mentally quiet, relaxing can, at times, seem threatening and even unpleasant. As a result, we often dismiss or even systematically avoid learning techniques for stress management. Eventually, though, we must develop ways of successfully dealing with stress, because this skill is absolutely essential for our physical and emotional health.

We should also take care to address problems in the area of our interpersonal skills. Clearly, triggered emotions from buried events cause us to overreact to minor interpersonal conflicts and concerns, which in itself can be terribly counterproductive to basic socializing. However, traumatic experiences also directly teach us unhealthy patterns of interacting, both by discouraging beneficial behaviors, such as the proper venting of anger, and by encouraging those that are inappropriate, such as excessive submissiveness. As a result, even after the past is processed, we may still be at a loss when we try to manage conflict, set healthy relational boundaries, and communicate our viewpoint and feelings.

These interpersonal shortcomings are especially troublesome in our interactions with our children. In part, this is because children lack interpersonal skills as well, but most of the trouble usually stems from a basic lack of knowledge about parenting. Since most of us learn to nurture and discipline children from our parents, those of us raised by parents who were abusive, or even just seriously limited, miss out on important lessons in this area. We may even come to associate discipline with abuse—an association that seriously interferes with our ability to provide the structure that our children desperately need—and unfortunately, this problem will not go away simply by working on the pain from our childhood. We must replace these missing skills directly.

In spite of this rather extensive list of potential problems, we should not be intimidated. Even in the worst scenarios, we learn some of these skills simply by a kind of osmosis, as we take in information about how other people cope, and we can talk with our counselor about how to fill the remaining gaps. Options include reading books, attending classes, approaching others for advice, and learning Dialectic Behavior Therapy (a treatment focused mainly on teaching coping skills). Also, if we feel comfortable in groups, this setting is wonderful for picking up parenting skills, social skills and certain techniques for stress management. We should keep in mind, however, that learning these skills takes time and can be frustrating and exhausting, at least initially. This is normal. Learning life skills is no different from learning to type or play a guitar. In order to accomplish each of these goals, we must practice, practice, and then practice some more.

REDISCOVERING THE SELF

The first time my therapist asked me to tell her what I liked about myself, it felt like she had asked me to explain the theory of relativity. Then she asked me just to tell her some of my qualities—how I would describe myself to a stranger. It seemed like such a simple question, but I went completely blank. I had spent the last

37 years in this body, with this personality, 24 hours a day, 7 days
a week, and I literally could not think of a single thing to say about
who I was—how weird is that?

—Gena J.

In working on the "damaged floorboards" of our psyche, there is one last critical area that still needs to be considered: our sense of self. Our perception of who we are—our attributes, personality quirks, interests, accomplishments and goals—normally develops without deliberate effort, but unchecked buried experiences can seriously distort our awareness of ourselves and what makes us tick. When anger, anxiety, depression, addictions and emotional chaos are a pervasive and persistent part of our life for decades, we learn to think of these problems as the core of our personality, confusing our identity with our symptoms.

As a result, when these symptoms improve, we may feel profound loss and confusion about our sense of self. If we are not the basket case we have always been, then who are we? Nature abhors a vacuum, and this is especially true in regard to our identity. The psyche will tolerate our inability to define who we are for only a short time. As a result, there is a very real danger that we will return to those dysfunctional behaviors unless we develop a healthier sense of self. We may go back to being a basket case simply to have a sense of self. As strange as it may sound, we may subconsciously choose to stay stuck in our old patterns to avoid having to look for new ones.

However, we do not need to fall into this trap if we know how to fill that void. Although we normally do not put conscious awareness or effort into our sense of identity, it is relatively easy to jump-start its development on a conscious level later in life. We simply need to intentionally explore several different aspects of our personality: our interests, accomplishments, qualities, skills and goals. In other words, we need to ask ourselves what we enjoy doing, whom we enjoy being around, what we have accomplished, what personality traits make us different from others, whether we have any special talents or abilities, and where we want to go in life.

On the other hand, as Gena found, these questions are not always easy to answer. Due to our psyche's intense fear that focusing inward will trigger buried memories, we often go blank when exploring these issues, but we should not be put off. With time and effort, the psyche's resistance will usually dissipate, and if simple persistence does not work, we can always talk to others about how they see us. As long as we agree with their opinion, we can include these items in our assessment of our self, but keep in mind that we must agree with their viewpoint—we should never try to adopt a sense of self that is not our own. Finally, once we have pinpointed some answers to these questions, we must be sure to write them down, so our psyche does not make them vanish once more.

The next step in developing our identity is to reinforce and broaden the interests, accomplishments, qualities and skills on our list. If we enjoyed certain activities as a child or young adult, we should try them again if at all possible. In addition to reconnecting with prior hobbies, we can celebrate the qualities that make us different from or connected to others. Expanding our repertoire of interests is a particularly effective way to nurture our identity, and there are many options from which to choose. To list just a few of many examples: someone with a genius IQ could join Mensa, those who are particularly caring often enjoy volunteering at a hospital or an animal shelter, and people who like the outdoors can hook up with a bird-watching group or a hiking club.

However, engaging in these various activities may initially feel awkward or embarrassing. We might think that we are too old to reconnect with former interests or to explore new hobbies. At first, making a model

EXERCISE 10 - 2

Your coping skills and sense of identity are critical to the healing process. Be absolutely certain that you have taken the necessary steps to ensure that they are not overlooked during your recovery. Go over these areas with a fine-tooth comb: your ability to manage the entire range of emotions, your ability to deal with stress, your interpersonal skills, and your ability to recognize the qualities that make you a unique individual. Identify the areas most in need of work and talk with your counselor about the best options for addressing those shortfalls.

airplane or flying a kite can feel silly, but play is rejuvenating and healthy, regardless of our age. Sometimes, our discomfort is more deeply rooted; being present to ourselves again after decades of being away can be incredibly painful. However, if we move through this discomfort, we should find that the energy we put into these interests and activities provides a tremendous sense of well-being and renewal. By reinforcing our individuality, remembering our past and celebrating our passions, we nurture a healthy, positive sense of identity.

THE BIG PICTURE OF HEALING

> *When I started counseling, I didn't realize how much I was being affected by the things I had been through. I thought it was just the panic. I know it sounds stupid but I wanted the counselor to wave a magic wand and make the panic go away and I'd be done—keep it simple and fix it. But it didn't take long for me to see that there was more going on. I hadn't been sleeping right for decades, had no friends, couldn't assert myself to save my life—literally, no ambition, no joy. I was just existing. I wanted a bandage. I needed major surgery.*
>
> —*Ron H.*

Although healing does not need to be complicated, it is a multi-faceted process. Clearly, being able to control or eliminate problematic feelings, thoughts and memories is a priority. For this task, we can use the various aspects of our self—our emotions, thoughts, behaviors, capacity for insight, subconscious abilities and innate physiological responses—to help our psyche finish the integration, storage and avoidance of buried unprocessed events. However, unless we are dealing with a particularly painful *recent* event, these experiences cannot be our *total* focus—not even initially.

When grappling with a backlog of memories, we also need to simultaneously evaluate our relationships and spirituality, acquire missing life skills, and rediscover our lost sense of identity. Since problems in any of these areas can sabotage our recovery, we must be sure to address these resources and skills while we battle the monsters in our closet. This requires quite a bit of juggling. Usually we will need to alternate between dealing with past experiences, addressing the current situation and filling voids in our sense of self, skills and relationships. To demonstrate how these different issues interact, let's look at a particularly challenging example of this process: recovery from addiction.

ADDICTION RECOVERY

> *Getting sober made me feel like a fish learning to live out of water. The first step was believing that I even could, but it didn't get much easier from there. Everything about how I lived and func-tioned had to change. But if I was going to evolve, there really wasn't much choice, was there?*
>
> —*Darrell M.*

As we know, addictions are an incredibly common way for the sub-conscious to keep overwhelming experiences out of awareness. As a result, it is highly likely that, at some point, each of us will deal with addic-tions in one form or another, from minor distractions to hard-core drug addiction. Unfortunately, their near-inevitability does not make addictions any easier to overcome. Because our addictive patterns often serve as the lynchpin that holds us together, addressing them is not only a vital part of the healing process, but it is also one that requires facing a variety of issues simultaneously. In other words, overcoming addictions necessitates using all the different aspects of healing that we have just discussed.

Since much of the addictive drive is rooted in the need to bury unprocessed experiences, we might reasonably assume that the first step in recovery is resolving these experiences. However, addressing our past, while avoiding relapse in the present, is not as straightforward as it might seem. Integrating buried events ultimately eases our addictive drive, but unfortunately, processing also inevitably stirs up painful feelings, which increases the risk of relapse. Ironically, therefore, working to overcome our addictive drive by processing the past can cause us to relapse—making addiction recovery seem like a Catch-22.

Some of us resolve this dilemma by simply ignoring the past, but dismissing our history has a downside as well. Like it or not, eliminating an addiction allows buried memories to surface. At some point in recovery, unless we pick a new addiction, we can count on being flooded with old overwhelming data. This flood may happen at the very beginning of recovery or after years of sobriety. It can happen for no reason at all or due to a particular trigger, such as the death of an abusive parent. It can involve complete memories or just random fragments without any information about their source. While we may try to prevent, or at least minimize, this surge of memories by doing as much anticipatory work as possible, sobriety often unearths issues that we did not even know existed.

It is best, therefore, during the early stages of recovery, to prepare for this flood by building a healthy support system and finding a counselor we can trust. Discussing our story with a counselor early in the recovery process gives us someone we can turn to in a crisis and also makes it easier to work on our past when we are ready. At some point in our healing, we will learn to manage the relapse urges that accessing old memories and feelings brings up. Ultimately, those urges will diminish, but initially, this process can be incredibly perilous. Taking the steps of developing a healthy support group and connecting with a counselor eases that danger. If we are prepared and have the proper assistance, we can deal with our past without sabotaging our sobriety.

Facing the issues in our closet, however, is not the only area of addiction recovery that requires extra precautions. We must also pay close attention to the psyche's defenses, which will attempt—often very convincingly—to persuade us to relapse. As we know, our psyche protects and justifies addictions in its efforts to keep our issues buried. To accomplish this goal, it will use every possible rationalization for relapse. Addressing this "addictive voice," as it is known in Rational Recovery, is an extremely important aspect of our recovery. Although we cannot go into the details of this problem here, *Rational Recovery: The New Cure for Substance Addiction* by Jack Trimpey provides some excellent potential solutions.

Finally, as is necessary for recovery from all emotional problems, we need to look for problems in the areas of our support system, coping skills and identity, since these aspects of our lives can sabotage our healing even if we are making terrific headway otherwise. In particular, as mentioned earlier, we will need to make serious changes in our support system, perhaps even give up some of our closest friends. For many of us, letting go of relationships with people who cannot support us in our efforts to heal is the most difficult part of recovery. Fortunately, addictions-centered groups, such as Alcoholics Anonymous or therapist-run support groups, are excellent resources for developing new friendships that will help us deal with the challenges of staying sober.

As we may expect, juggling the many interconnected tasks of healing can initially be exhausting, but these interconnections can also be a plus, because progress in one area will speed progress in others. Before long, as we grapple with the various facets of healing, our ability to function in healthy ways will return. Like an atrophied limb that is being rehabilitated, our psyche will begin to revive. Having repaired the damage from the past, we are now free to focus on the future. It would be a shame to see our newly cleaned out—or reorganized—closet filled again with another backlog of beasties. Fortunately, our newfound knowledge about how the psyche works gives us a number of terrific options for preventing new monsters from creeping in.

Chapter Eleven

PREVENTION: MASTERING POTENTIAL MONSTERS

*Rest is not idleness, and to lie sometimes on the grass under trees
on a summer's day, listening to the murmur of the water or watching clouds float across the sky, is by no means a waste of time.*
—*Sir John Lubbock*

The sense of liberation that comes from regaining control over our
emotions and mastering self-destructive habits is like recovering
the ability to walk after years of paralysis. However, as in the
case of physical injury and illness, avoiding problems in the first place is
infinitely preferable. On a physical level, we do this by taking advantage
of nutritious foods, exercise, and safety devices, like airbags and seat
belts, and we seek appropriate treatment when trouble does occur.
Emotionally, we have ways to avoid injury as well and, when ordeals happen, to intervene quickly and effectively in order to prevent long-term
damage.

Today, our knowledge of how the mind works can help us not only to
resolve issues from the past but also prevent overwhelming events from
affecting our mental health in the future. We are now able to recognize

experiences that create emotional problems and can address them promptly, in the same way that we quickly seek help for broken bones or serious cuts. However, knowing when to seek immediate treatment is only one aspect of prevention. To really care for our emotional health, we must also nurture and strengthen our psyche, thereby building its resistance to emotional problems. In this way, we can decrease our susceptibility to trauma and limit the damage caused by life's periodic ordeals.

ANTICIPATING INTEGRATION FAILURES

When I read about people surviving something really terrible, like a kidnapping or a serious earthquake, I can't help wondering what happens afterwards. Sure they survived physically, but what about the rest of the story? Are they going to get the help they need to really make it back? You hear about so many survivors of major catastrophes falling apart afterwards. Isn't it time for people to realize that just because it's over, it's not necessarily over?
—Ginnie B.

One critical component of emotional self-care is identifying potentially overwhelming events when they *first* happen. Although integration failures are difficult to anticipate, we can be extra vigilant during certain high-risk times. For example, we now know that processing problems are more likely to happen when we are extremely tired or must process large amounts of new information. We can also recognize the definitive signs of trouble with integration, such as dreaming or thinking excessively about what happened, or wanting to avoid thinking about the event. Finally, we understand that we must seek help immediately whenever we feel as if we are having a nervous breakdown or that we want to die.

We also need to remember, when looking for potentially overwhelming events, that it is critical to determine our level of processing—our *individual* ability to integrate experiences—and that in making this assessment, it is important to distinguish between a talent for stuffing and the ability to integrate events easily. We must keep in mind that apathy and emotional indifference are indications of avoidance, not integration. It is only when we can *comfortably* talk about a painful event, and are aware of how it made us feel, that we have truly finished integration. If we find ourselves repeatedly avoiding discussing difficult times or are unable to acknowledge our emotions about those experiences, we should consider the possibility that these events have not been processed, and this indicates something about our overall processing abilities.

While it is important that we be aware of any trouble we may experience with integration, being a low processor does not necessarily need to affect our quality of life. Just as awareness of a genetic predisposition for diabetes simply means being more vigilant about sugar intake, being aware of a low processing ability merely means that we must be sure to put in the effort necessary to completely integrate moderately—and for some of us, minimally—disturbing incidents. By being familiar with our level of processing, taking extra precautions during times of high risk, and knowing the signs that our psyche is struggling with integration, we can prevent problems from developing and effectively protect our emotional health.

EXERCISE 11 - 1

Think about your individual level of processing and some of the events that you have been through in the past couple of years. With the help of your counselor, try to determine approximately how well your psyche seems to handle difficult experiences and identify some of the ways you react when you are overwhelmed. Then discuss options for dealing with these events in the future, such as keeping a journal, doing physical exercise, or hashing things out with a close friend. Be sure that you are able to find alternatives that fit your particular personality and coping style but that also help you finish processing.

THE CHALLENGES OF CHILDHOOD

My son has had problems with grief ever since our dog died three years ago. Any time he has to deal with a loss or a change, he just loses it. When we had to move, he nearly had to be hospitalized. If

he has to say good-bye to a favorite teacher at the end of the school
year, he's hell on wheels for months afterwards. It's hard to believe
that a small thing like our dog's death has affected him so severe-
ly, but that dog was his life before it died. I guess when you're a
child, you have more trouble with that sort of thing.

—Amy E.

There is a common misperception in our culture that children "bounce back" easily from trauma. This misconception is rooted in the effortlessness with which children are able to push disturbing memories into their relatively empty trauma closets. However, we should not confuse a knack for repression with integration. The reality is that painful experiences are, for the most part, much more difficult for children to process, because they have a limited frame of reference and minimal coping skills. As a result, their capacity to integrate intense events is not the same as an adult's, and their talent for repression means they will be affected by these unprocessed events for years to come. However, we can keep this from happening by taking a few simple steps to help our children deal with painful experiences.

The first and most crucial step is to counter the cultural norms encouraging our children—or anyone—to shut down their emotions. It is critical to realize that telling a child to "be strong" during a particularly painful event is like telling someone with a broken bone to "shake it off." The child who grits his teeth and finishes out a Little League game on a fractured ankle, because he is afraid to disappoint his coach, is likely to end up with a much more severe injury. Likewise, the child who believes that she will disappoint her parents if she expresses anger about leaving a beloved home will often face more serious consequences down the road. To prevent this, we must teach children the importance of processing disturbing events and feelings before they become buried.

Helping children deal with painful events also means paying attention to their reactions and recognizing when they are having trouble coping. If we notice they are having difficulty with being bullied by an older child or with feeling betrayed by a best friend, we need to walk them through the expression process. Because children can be confused by the differences between emotions, we often have to first help them identify what they are feeling. Then, we need to teach them to express themselves and show them appropriate ways to vent. In the process, we give them a safe, acceptable release for emotions and demonstrate that feelings are important, and valid, but also manageable. Most importantly, they learn that it is possible to achieve closure.

In addition to encouraging children to properly express their emotions, we also need to explain what is happening and why things occurred. These explanations give children a frame of reference that keeps them from being confused, especially about the issue of blame. Because normal developmental patterns predispose children to feel guilty for negative events, such as abuse or their parents' divorce, they tend to take on excessive responsibility during difficult times. Even in cases of serious abuse, a simple explanation—such as the reassurance, "it's not your fault, you did nothing wrong"—given as quickly as possible after the traumatic event can help minimize their guilt and shame.

Sometimes, keeping an experience from affecting a child means seeking the help of a trained counselor. Although talking with children and teaching them to recognize and appropriately express emotions is often sufficient, some experiences will simply be too painful to work through in this manner. We must watch for the signs that a child is being seriously affected. When he or she obsesses about a situation, avoids talking about it altogether, or displays drastic changes in mood, behavior, or sleep patterns, it is highly likely that the child's integration abilities have been overwhelmed. In these cases, it is generally a good idea to contact a counselor who can help.

RELAXATION

I've been taking meditation classes for about 6 months now, and I can't believe the difference they're making. I feel like a new person. I'm so much more centered and connected. I've been wanting to take a class for years and I just never got around to it. Isn't it funny how we prioritize painting the bedrooms or watching television over something that makes us feel truly alive?

—Michaela B.

Strengthening the psyche to increase its resilience is another way we can attempt to prevent emotional problems—for example, through relaxation. Just as quality sleep, exercise and nutritious food strengthen our body so that it can resist injuries and illness, "down time" naturally helps our psyche resist being overwhelmed. Relaxation exercises, meditation, yoga and prayer rejuvenate our mind so it can function effectively and complete unfinished processing. However, those of us totally unaccustomed to relaxing may not even know how to begin. Fortunately, *The Relaxation and Stress Reduction Workbook,* by Davis, McKay and Eshelman, offers a wide range of alternatives to get us started.

When beginning a relaxation program, however, we must remember that the psyche will fight any activity that is likely to bring buried memories to the surface. So we should develop a plan to counteract possible problems with avoidance. For example, we can use behavioral reinforcement to encourage maintaining a relaxation routine, or we can list the benefits of relaxation—that it enhances our physical health, allows us to access and process experiences more effectively, and decreases the likelihood of being overwhelmed by new experiences (Freinkel, 2000). We must also make arrangements for dealing with any feelings and memories that do surface. Although relaxing may not be as simple as we would like, once past these initial obstacles, we will most likely wonder, like Michaela, why we waited so long.

OVERCOMING OVERSTIMULATION

> *Some days, I'm so busy I don't even know who I am. I feel like a robot on an assembly line: do this—now do that—now the next thing. I can't keep up. How am I supposed to find time to relax? And the truth is that even when I do have a few minutes, I still can't slow down. My brain is in overdrive and a little peace and quiet is not going to change that. I'm on a treadmill with no way off.*
> —Ruth L.

For many of us, cluttered schedules and lack of stress management know-how are not the only obstacles to relaxation. Often, the biggest barrier is the fact that we have become accustomed to constant stimulation. In today's world, music comes at us continually—at home, in stores, in our cars, even in elevators. There are billboards and bumper stickers to read as we drive, and phone calls to make and receive at any time or place. Many of us find it impossible to sleep if we cannot hear the noise of a radio or television. We remain so busy that even our vacations are jammed with "recreation." As a result, we never stop to face ourselves, our emotions and our experiences. We never deal with us.

This constant activity is common for adults, and it is even more of a problem with children. In today's world, most children spend their free time playing video games, watching television or participating in structured sports. Rather than helping with processing, the constant need to pay attention, and in some cases the persistent demand for an immediate response, recreates exactly that sense of "crisis" that so effectively suspends integration and interferes with the psyche's ability to work through life's lessons and experiences. The relentless pressure, intensity and suspense of these activities may be doing wonders for our children's reflexes, but this form of "leisure" is wreaking havoc on our children's tension levels and denying them opportunities to integrate life events.

Even for adults, continual stimulation is incredibly destructive. The human psyche relies on moments of peace to process both day-to-day and more disturbing experiences. It desperately needs time away from activity, work, and distraction: not in front of a television, or even a book, but true mental relaxation. It may sound cliché, but time spent on a front-porch swing, sleeping in a hammock, or staring at the stars is critical to our mental health. Even when these quiet times make us feel

EXERCISE 11 - 2

Disconnecting from cultural pressures to maintain an over-stimulated lifestyle and developing the ability to relax are absolutely critical to your mental and emotional health. Talk with your counselor about ways to include relaxation in your day-to-day life, and discuss options for clearing excess stimulation from your life if this is a problem area.

bored and uncomfortable, we cannot let our psyche fool us. Like an exhausted child who throws a tantrum when told to go to bed, the busy person who tries to relax, only to be plagued by feelings of boredom, is really over-tired: what is needed is more rest, not more stimulation.

RECLAIMING OUR MENTAL HEALTH

It feels so wonderful to know that no matter what happens I can deal with it. It's an incredible feeling knowing that I can get over anything life dishes out. I've had to face a lot of difficult feelings, and it's been painful. But it was so worth it! There's nothing that compares with leaving the past in the past, and knowing that no matter what happens in the future, I can get through it. I'll survive and be stronger because of it.

—Lisa B.

We have become a society that expects emotional turbulence. We think that stress, tension and hectic schedules are unavoidable, and we accept emotional chaos as a fact of life. Like learning to live with a limp, we have adjusted to the irrational responses and destructive behaviors that are rampant in our world today. In our "modern" eyes, the dysfunctional family is normal, abuse is routine, and addictions are unavoidable. Individually, we may do battle with our out-of-control emotions and behaviors, but as a society, we have come to believe that self-destructive responses are commonplace and inescapable.

However, a future of emotional illness and distress is not inevitable. We cannot stop painful, even destructive, events from happening, any more than we can prevent all physical injuries. There will always be times when we become overwrought, but just as we can take steps to care for our physical health in the face of accidents and illness, we can also protect our emotional health from periodic traumas. We can relax and put limits on stimulation, so our psyche is prepared for ordeals, and we can recognize situations that have surpassed our integration abilities and get the appropriate help.

162

Every one of us was born free from monsters, with our psyche's closet empty of pain. There was a time in each of our lives when we were not fettered by unresolved buried issues. We are all capable of being those people again—truly alive and joyful once more. By taking the steps necessary to prevent emotional problems from developing and by dealing with any issues that happen to accumulate, we can experience the peace of truly putting the past in the past. We can let go of our most painful and disabling emotional problems and be free to respond in healthy and productive ways.

If this vision of life without dysfunctional families and emotional turmoil sounds impossibly utopian, we should remember that not much more than a century ago, a simple cut or a minor cold could have been a death sentence. It was only when scientists, doctors and everyday laypeople learned about germs and how to fight them that we were able to conquer these once-fatal infections. Our new understanding of non-integrated events can have an equally significant impact on our emotional well-being. Armed with an awareness of how these events contribute to emotional problems and the tools to help the psyche complete its tasks, we are finally able to properly care for our mental health. Dying from suicide or addiction can become as uncommon as dying from a cold or an infected cut is today. At last, we have the ability to master our monsters and truly live.

BIBLIOGRAPHY

American Psychiatric Association. (1994) *Diagnostic and Statistical Manual of Mental Disorders,* 4th ed. Washington, D.C: American Psychiatric Association.

Azar, S., and C. Twentyman. (1986) Cognitive-Behavioral Perspectives in the Assessment and Treatment of Child Abuse. In P. Kendall (ed.), *Advances in Cognitive-Behavioral Research and Therapy,* vol 5. London: Academic Press.

Beitman, B., M. Goldfried, and J. Norcross. (1989) The Movement toward Integrating the Psychotherapies: An Overview. *American Journal of Psychiatry* 146: 138-147.

Bisbey, L. (1995) No Longer a Victim: A Treatment Outcome Study of Crime Victims with Post-Traumatic Stress Disorder. Doctoral dissertation, California School of Professional Psychology, San Diego, CA.

Bradshaw, J. (1990) *Homecoming: Reclaiming and Championing Your Inner Child.* New York: Bantam Books.

Burns, D. (1999) *The Feeling Good Handbook.* New York: Penguin Putnam.

——— (2000) Strategies for Therapeutic Success. Seminar held in Tucson, AZ, October 8-9.

Callahan, R. (1996) *Thought Field Therapy (TFT) and Trauma: Treatment and Theory.* Indian Wells, CA: Thought Field Therapy Training Center.

——— (2001) The Impact of Thought Field Therapy on Heart Rate Variability (HRV). *Journal of Clinical Psychology* 57 (10): 1153-1170.

Capacehione, L. (2001) *The Power of Your Other Hand: A Course in Channeling the Inner Wisdom of the Right Brain.* Franklin Lakes, NJ: New Page Books.

Chemtob, C.M., D.F. Tolin, B.A. van der Kolk, and R.K. Pitman. (2000) Eye Movement Desensitization and Reprocessing (EMDR). *In* Foa, E.B., T. Keane, and M. Friedman, (eds.) *ISTSS guidelines for PTSD.* New York: Guilford Press.

Coughlin, W. (1995) Traumatic Incident Reduction: Efficacy in Reducing Anxiety Symptomatology. Doctoral dissertation, Union Institute, Cincinnati, OH. Order #9537919.

Craig, G., and A. Fowlie. (1995) *Emotional Freedom Techniques.* Self-published.

Davis, M., M. McKay, and E. Eschelman. (2003) *The Relaxation and Stress Reduction Workbook.* New York: MJF Books.

Della Selva, P. (1996) *Intensive Short-term Dynamic Psychotherapy: Theory and Technique.* New York: John Wiley & Sons.

Ellis, A. (1999) *How to Make Yourself Happy and Remarkably Less Disturbable.* Atascadero, CA: Impact Publishers Inc.

Freinkel, S. (2000) An Unforgettable Reason to Relax. *Health,* March 70-74.

Freinkel, S., M. Fuerst, and E. Krieger. (1999) The Write Way to Get Healthy. *Health,* July/August 30.

Geen, R., and M. Quanty. (1977) The Catharsis of Aggression: An Evaluation of Hypothesis. *In* L. Berkowitz (ed.), *Advances in Experimental Social Psychology,* vol. 10. New York: Academic Press

Gendlin, E. (1979) Experiential Psychotherapy. In R. Corsini (ed.), *Current Psychotherapies.* Itasca, IL: F. E. Peacock Publishers.

Kihlstrom, J., and W. Nasby. (1981) Cognitive Tasks in Clinical Assessment: An Exercise in Applied Psychology. *In* Kendall, P., and S. Hollon (eds.), *Assessment Strategies for Cognitive-Behavioral Interventions.* New York: Academic Press.

Levy, D. (1976) Release Therapy. *In* C. Schaefer (ed.), *The Therapeutic Use of Child's Play.* Northvale, NJ: Jason Aronson Inc.

Malan, D. (1976) *Toward the Validation of Dynamic Psychotherapy.* New York: Plenum Medical Book Co.

Mosak, H. (1979) Adlerian Psychotherapy. *In* R. Corsini (ed.), *Current Psychotherapies.* Itasca, IL: F. E. Peacock Publishers.

Myers, D. (1998) *Psychology,* 5th ed. New York: Worth Publishers.

Oaklander, V. (1978) *Windows to Our Children.* Moab, UT: Real People Press.

Rothbaum, B.O. (1997) A Controlled Study of Eye Movement Desensitization and Reprocessing for Posttraumatic Stress Disordered Sexual Assault Victims. *Bulletin of the Menninger Clinic* 61: 317-334.

Shapiro, F. (1995) *Eye Movement Desensitization and Reprocessing: Basic Principles, Protocols, and Procedures.* New York: Guilford Press.

Spradlin, S. (2003) *Don't Let Your Emotions Run Your Life: How Dialectical Behavioral Therapy Can Put You in Control*. Oakland, CA: New Harbinger Publications.

Stafford, M. (1999) Personal interview, May.

Tavris, C. (1982) Anger Defused. *Psychology Today,* November 25-35.

Trimpey, J. (1996) *Rational Recovery: The New Cure for Substance Addiction*. New York: Pocket Books.

Whitfield, C. (1987) *Healing the Child Within: Discovery and Recovery for Adult Children of Dysfunctional Families*. Deerfield Beach, FL: HCI Publishing.

Wilson, S.A., L.A. Becker, and R.H. Tinker. (1995) Eye Movement Desenstization and Reprocessing (EMDR) Treatment for Psychologically Traumatized Individuals. *Journal of Consulting and Clinical Psychology* 63: 928-937.

—— (1997) Fifteen-month Follow-up of Eye Movment Desensitization and Reprocessing (EMDR) Treatment for Posttraumatic Stress Disorder and Psychological Trauma. *Journal of Consulting and Clinical Psychology* 65(6): 1047-1056.

Wylie, M.S. (1996) Researching PTSD: Going for the Cure. *The Family Therapy Networker* 20 (4), 20-37.

Zastrow, C. (1981) *The Practice of Social Work*. Homewood, IL: The Dorsey Press.

INDEX

ORDER FORM

To request additional copies of *The Monsters in Our Closets*,

FAX your order to: 1-520-326-0269. Send this form.

TELEPHONE your order to: 1-520-326-0269. Please have your credit card ready.

INTERNET orders possible at blinkinglightpublishing.com.

MAIL your order to: Blinking Light Publishing, P.O. Box 27503A, Tucson, AZ, 85726-7503.

Name _____

Address _____

City _____ State _____ Zip _____

Country _____

E-mail address _____

Sales tax:
Please add $1.04 per item for books shipped to Arizona addresses.

Shipping:
US: $4.95 for first book and $2.00 for each additional copy.
International: $9.50 for first book and $5.00 for each additional copy (United States currency).

For bulk orders (10 or more copies), please place your order through the website address above.

Payment:
    □ VISA   □ MC   □ Discover   □ AmEx   □ Personal check

Name on card:_____

Card Number_____

Expiration Date _____

www.ingramcontent.com/pod-product-compliance
Lightning Source LLC
Chambersburg PA
CBHW031202270326
41931CB00006B/367